Mental Dynamics

Mental
Dynamics

Power Thinking
for Personal Success

K. Thomas Finley

PRENTICE HALL
Paramus, New Jersey 07652

Library of Congress Cataloging-in-Publication Data

Finley, K. Thomas (Kay Finley), 1934–.
    Mental dynamics : power thinking for personal success / K. Thomas
Finley.—2nd ed.
      p. cm.
    Includes index.
    ISBN 0-13-566431-4
    1. Mental discipline.   2. Success—Psychological aspects.
I. Title.
BF632.F5 1991   90-38372
153.4′2—dc20   CIP

© *1996, 1991 by Prentice-Hall, Inc.*

All rights reserved. No part of this book may be reproduced in any form or by any means, without permission in writing from the publisher.

Printed in the United States of America

20 19 18 17 16 15 14 13 12 11

This book is a reference work based on research by the author. The opinions expressed herein are not necessarily those of or endorsed by the Publisher.

ISBN 0-13-566431-4

ATTENTION: CORPORATIONS AND SCHOOLS

Prentice Hall books are available at quantity discounts with bulk purchase for educational, business, or sales promotional use. For information, please write to: Prentice Hall Special Sales, 240 Frisch Court, Paramus, New Jersey 07652. Please supply: title of book, ISBN number, quantity, how the book will be used, date needed.

PRENTICE HALL
Paramus, NJ 07652

A Simon & Schuster Company

On the World Wide Web at http://www.phdirect.com

Prentice-Hall International (UK) Limited, *London*
Prentice-Hall of Australia Pty. Limited, *Sydney*
Prentice-Hall Canada Inc., *Toronto*
Prentice-Hall Hispanoamericana, S.A., *Mexico*
Prentice-Hall of India Private Limited, *New Delhi*
Prentice-Hall of Japan, Inc., *Tokyo*
Simon & Schuster Asia Pte. Ltd., *Singapore*
Editora Prentice-Hall do Brasil, Ltda., *Rio de Janeiro*

What This Book Will Do for You

What is the *real* secret of success? Is it personality? Is it heredity? Is it education? All these are a part of it, of course, but there is something more important than any of them—the ability to think. The person who is truly able to learn, to reason, to remember is the absolute master of his or her own life.

And you don't have to be a genius to use your brains effectively. Look at the men and women around you. Most of them are ordinary people. Few of them have towering IQs. Still, those who have achieved their goals in life are almost sure to be the ones who can and do use their minds to best advantage.

Leaders in every field, from skilled labor to nuclear research, have this one ability in common: They are able to think with greater speed, accuracy, and simple horse sense than those around them. They have learned the best ways to acquire and retain information. There is no substititue for this ability—not looks, not personality, not influential friends. In the last analysis, it is mental skill that pays off on most jobs.

The purpose of this book is to map out a common-sense program for effective thinking. This is the first time that speed reading, vocabulary building, mental arithmetic, ideation, and the rest have been set forth and explained as a single system.

The book begins with the birth of thought, which is motivation, and ends with the culmination of effective thought, which is leadership. It is broken into three logical parts: (1) The Dynamics of Learning, (2) The Dynamics of Memory, and (3) The Dynamics of Critical and Creative Thought. Each part is further broken down into related but semi-independent chapters.

There is a minimum of theory here. The book deals with specifics. Designed as a practical guide to the subject of human thought, it contains proven and usable techniques on how to learn, how to remember, and how to think critically and creatively. It avoids academic jargon, yet it is based on scholarship as well as firsthand experience.

The book should be valuable reading for anyone whose job involves mental effort. And whose job doesn't?

Contents

Part 1

The Dynamics of Learning

As a field, however fertile,
cannot be fruitful without
cultivation, neither can a
mind without learning.

—CICERO

Chapter 1

The Principles of Power Thinking

- The Importance of Experience
- Cherchez le Word
- Use Your Common Sense
- Apply What You Already Know
- What Do You Read?
- Cow_1 Is Not Cow_2
- Building the Foundation
- Ten Tips for Power Thinking

Nот LONG AGO, A FRIEND OF MINE was showing me his new car. He lifted the hood, glanced lovingly at the engine, and asked me, "What do you think about *that?*"

The proper answer, which I didn't give him, was that I thought nothing at all about it. To me an engine is an engine; I am not interested in automotive mechanics, and my experience with engines is extremely limited.

Suppose I had brought my friend into a chemistry classroom, written $C_9H_8O_4$ on the chalkboard, and asked him, "What do you think about *that?*" What would his reply have been? Probably he would have answered that he didn't know what $C_9H_8O_4$ is.

Yet day after day, people are put into somewhat similar situations, and they almost never give the most obvious and honest answer. For example, how would you respond to these questions: "What do you think about nuclear power?" "What do you think about the foreign aid bill?" "What do you think about the sales potential of microwidgets?"

With rare exceptions, the proper answer would be, "My experience is too limited for me to make a reliable judgment." This does not mean that you do not, or should not, have opinions on the subjects. It simply means that to some extent you, like most people, will be talking from partial ignorance. You should be aware of the limitation, *and you should admit the limitation when you express an opinion.* As Mark Twain said, "This will gratify some people and astonish the rest."

THE IMPORTANCE OF EXPERIENCE

Before you can think clearly and deeply about any subject, you must have some experience with it. The more experience you have, generally speaking, the more reliable your judgments will

5

be. This experience can be gained in three ways: (1) by personal observation, (2) by listening, and (3) by reading.

When a doctor states her opinion of a patient's chances for recovery, her judgment is likely to be highly reliable, for her experience with the subject matter is broad. But when the same doctor is asked her opinion of the outcome of a mayoral election in, say, San Antonio, two thousand miles away, her judgment—if she tries to give one—will probably be less reliable than a small-town politician's from Texas. Experience is the essential difference.

When Benjamin Franklin said, "Experience keeps a dear school, but fools will learn in no other," he was limiting his definition of experience. A baby who touches a hot stove is not considered a fool for doing so; the baby is simply a person without experience. When a grown man touches a stove even though someone tells him it is hot, he is indeed a fool. He is a fool because he has disregarded his experience—his own experience with hot stoves, and the experience he acquired on being told that the stove was hot.

Under a modern definition of experience, therefore, Franklin's proverb would have to become: "Experience keeps a dear school, *but there is no other*."

The most common source of mistaken judgments is simply lack of experience. In many areas of knowledge, you have not seen enough, heard enough, or read enough to make a reliable judgment. In a world of proliferating knowledge, this is no disgrace. It is a far worse disgrace from the standpoint of power thinking to *pretend* that you have knowledge you do not have.

To summarize, knowledge comes from experience. It is gained through observing, listening, and reading. If your experience is broad, you should not hesitate to make reasoned judgments. If your experience is limited, you should not hesitate to express opinions—but you should frankly admit your limitations and recognize the possible error of your opinions.

CHERCHEZ LE WORD

We know that knowledge comes from experience. But even today, despite extensive research, psychologists cannot describe the exact process by which people think, nor do they know precisely how people learn. Witness their continuing debate over the value of intelligence tests. Witness their violent arguments over the look-say versus phonic method of teaching reading.

Still, there are hopeful signs. One of the most hopeful comes from the branch of linguistics called *semantics*, a study dealing with the nature of language. Semanticists emphasize a point which, at first glance, seems like an obvious truth: You think with words. This point actually has deep implications, for if you think with words, you must know the meanings of the words you use. Otherwise, you cannot think clearly.

But, you say to yourself, "I know the meanings of the words I use." Do you, though? Let's take one example: the word *wealth*. Can you define the word? Is it a "favorable" word to you or an "unfavorable" one? Where did you acquire your definition? (You certainly didn't look it up in the dictionary, today, yesterday, or ever!)

When a stockbroker thinks of *wealth,* does she have the same kind of mental image—the same definition, really—that a homeless person would have? Or that a single mother on welfare would have? Or that a delegate to the U. N. from a third-world country would have? Certainly not. The very meaning of *wealth* depends on the user's experience, his prejudices, his hopes, his fears.

This dual point—that (a) we think with words and (b) words do not mean the same thing to different people—is immensely important. You cannot talk sensibly or write rationally unless you understand it. The continuing debate over who or what is a "moderate" Republican illustrates the point perfectly. Everyone is in her own eyes a moderate, because he word *connotes* a common-sense, middle-of-the-road approach to politics, an approach that seems desirable. It *denotes* almost nothing—and a dictionary definition will not help you over such treacherous ground as this.

In stressing the difficulty of defining words, nearly every semanticist is fond of quoting from those most adult of children's books, *Alice in Wonderland* and *Through the Looking-Glass.* A favorite quotation is this:

> "But 'glory' doesn't mean 'a nice knock-down argument, ' " Alice objected.
>
> "When *I* use a word," Humpty Dumpty said in a rather scornful tone, "it means just what I choose it to mean— neither more nor less."

"The question is," said Alice, "whether you *can* make words mean so many different things."

"The question is," said Humpty Dumpty, "which is to be master—that's all."

The real question, of course, is whether you or your listeners know what you are talking about when you use certain words. *Wealth,* as you have seen, can cause trouble; so can *moderate*; so can *glory*; and so can many other words.

If you are to improve your ability to think clearly and to talk sensibly, you must begin by considering the meanings of words. The next time you argue with someone, try to "hear" not only the other person's words, but also his meanings. See if he himself really *knows* what he means when using certain hard-to-define words.

Remember that even a simple word like *house* does not have exactly the same meaning for a person in Beverly Hills that it has for me in Rochester, New York. Yet *house* is a *concrete* word and will cause few arguments. But when you use *abstract* words like *patriotism, honor, fair play, our way of life,* and so on, communication can fail miserably. The speaker may be talking about something totally different from what the listener thinks he is talking about.

Broad experience coupled with an ability to use words accurately constitutes a giant first step toward power thinking.

USE YOUR COMMON SENSE ══════════════

When you have sufficient experience from which to draw conclusions and when you have the right words with which to describe this experience, you are on your way to becoming a power thinker. However, other factors contribute to power thinking. One is common sense. Common sense has been described by Stuart Chase, a semanticist, as the sense that tells you the world is flat. This definition has an element of truth, but only a very small element.

Power thinking demands the application of old experience to new circumstances. You already know it is foolish to form conclusions, to make judgments, on the basis of too little experience. But how about people who have plenty of experience and still reach wrong conclusions? How about the cases where common sense must supplement, or even supplant, experience?

The point to be considered is this: Rely on your own experience. If, however, your experience seems contrary to common sense, follow your common sense. Occasionally you may conclude, with Stuart Chase, that the world is flat. But usually you will not go astray by putting common sense ahead of experience that seems to be misleading.

APPLY WHAT YOU ALREADY KNOW

All of us have some experience. Most of us have an adequate vocabulary for expressing our ideas. Most of us have some degree of common sense. Yet people still write to "Dear Abby," asking her how to order their personal lives. People still buy stock in nonexistent gold mines. People still try to beat the roulette wheel at Las Vegas. Clearly, something is wrong.

What is wrong is that people sometimes fail to apply what they already know. Much of the value of education, it seems to me, is the *transfer of learning* it makes possible. Years ago in elementary school you found out that two oranges plus two oranges would give you four oranges. If today a mechanic tells you he has two wrenches in his tool box and two on the workbench, you don't scratch your head in bewilderment, wondering how many wrenches he has in all. You don't say, "Well, if the wrenches were oranges, I'd know there were four. But I've never added wrenches before." Throughout your life you have transferred your knowledge from one situation to another roughly similar one.

Transfer of learning may be much more complex than in the orange–wrenches example. It is when such transfer becomes harder and less obvious that the power thinker comes into her own. There is no way to describe how transfer will work in a particular situation. The best advice is this: Whenever you are faced with a problem—either in business or in social life—look for precedents from your own experience to guide you. Few problems are unique. Most can be analyzed in terms of previous experience.

You have often heard that there is no excuse for making the same mistake twice. Neither is there any excuse for making *almost* the same mistake twice. Learning from your past mistakes is the surest method of avoiding future ones.

WHAT DO YOU READ?

One of the most brilliant young politicians in the United States said: "I spend more time reading newspapers and magazines that oppose me than I do reading those that favor me." This politician is obviously a power thinker. He does what you should do. He already knows his *own* viewpoint, but he feels that he may not fully understand the viewpoint of his opponents—and he wants to learn. As a consequence, he does learn. He is an almost unbeatable debater, too, for he often knows his opponents' arguments as well as they themselves do. He is seldom uninformed, seldom misinformed.

Yet many people, in all walks of life, follow a course that is exactly the opposite of this. They read nothing unless it supports their present convictions, or else they read nothing that is not directly related to their job. By doing so, they stop learning. They become prey to every charlatan who has read more than they have, or they come under the sway of people who know *both* sides of an issue and can use whatever arguments suit their purposes.

As a power thinker, you cannot be narrow-minded, uninformed, or half-informed. You must have a broad range of interests and be able to see all sides of a question, an aim you cannot achieve by limiting your sources of information to one newspaper, one magazine, one trade journal, or one television program. Instead, you must actually seek out sources of information that disagree with you. Only in this way will you come to know enough to support your own ideas in a competitive and sometimes hostile world.

To do this, of course, you must know what sources of information agree or disagree with you. If your inquiry is limited to news magazines, you will find a few magazines on the far right of the political spectrum, a few on the far left, and a great many in the middle. You should sample as many of them as possible. If you are a liberal Democrat, you might try reading the *National Review*, a magazine of decidedly right-wing views. If you are a conservative Republican, you might try reading the *New Republic*, a magazine with a leftist viewpoint. In either case, you will probably discover cogent arguments that you never knew existed.

Don't think, incidentally, that if you read a news magazine with wide circulation—*Time, Newsweek,* or *U. S. News and*

World Report—you are necessarily getting a balanced, objective presentation of the news. No single source of information is wholly objective, no matter how hard it may try—and two of the three magazines mentioned certainly do not try. Time magazine, in fact, states that it does not try; the editors point out that they regard interpretation as a necessary function of a news magazine. Perhaps they are right, but regardless, you should draw your own conclusions only after careful analysis of Time and its competitors.

To repeat, you should actively seek out sources of information whose interpretations differ from your own. You should examine these sources carefully, with an open mind but a critical eye. You will probably still disagree with their interpretations, but you will no longer disagree blindly.

COW₁ IS NOT COW₂

As you examine sources of information, you will draw on all the devices of power thinking that have been mentioned so far. You will apply your experience to what you observe, read or hear. You will notice whether words are used accurately or loosely. You will use your common sense. You will apply to present and future situations the information that you obtain.

In addition to doing these things, you will guard against one of the most prevalent causes of faulty thinking—the belief, as the semanticists put it, that Cow_1 is Cow_2. In S. I. Hayakawa's *Language in Thought and Action* (New York: Harcourt, Brace & World, Inc., 1964) the point is made this way:

> Remember that practically all statements in ordinary conversation, debate, and public controversy taking the form: "Republicans are Republicans," "Business is business," "Boys will be boys," "Women drivers are women drivers," and so on, are not true. Let us put one of these back into a context in life.
>
> "I don't think we should go through with this deal, Bill. Is it altogether fair to the railroad company?"
>
> "Aw, forget it! *Business is business,* after all."
>
> Such an assertion, although it looks like a "simple statement of fact," is not simple and is not a statement of fact. The first "business" *denotes* transaction under discussion; the

second "business" invokes the *connotations* of the word. The sentence is a directive, saying, "Let us treat this transaction with complete disregard for considerations other than profit, as the word 'business' suggests."

There is a simple technique for preventing such directives from having their harmful effect on our thinking. It is the suggestion made by Korzybski that we add "index numbers" to our terms, thus: $Englishman_1$, $Englishman_2$, $Englishman_3$. . .; cow_1, cow_2, cow_3. . .; $Frenchman_1, Frenchman_2, Frenchman_3$. . .; $communist_1$, $communist_2$, $communist_3$. . .The terms of the classification tell us what the individuals in that class have in common; *the index numbers remind us of the characteristics left out.* A rule can then be formulated as general guide in all of our thinking and reading: Cow_1, *is not* Cow_2; Jew_1 *is not* Jew_2; $politician_1$ *is not* $politician_2$, *and so on.*

By following Hayakawa's advice, you can avoid making *glittering generalizations.* Whenever you are tempted to say the "Labor leaders are corrupt," or that "Salesmen are all drunken louts," you will remember that labor $leader_1$ is not labor $leader_2$, and that $salesperson_1$ is not $salesperson_2$. Only rarely can you say or imply that *all* the people in a particular group have a common trait. Usually you must qualify your general statements. You may say, for instance, "All labor leaders *that I have met* have been corrupt," or you may say, "*I consider most* salesmen to be drunken louts." Such qualifying words will often make your statements at least defensible.

The avoidance of glittering generalizations—of the implication that Cow_1 *is* Cow_2—is the mark of an educated person

BUILDING THE FOUNDATION

Although not a great deal can be said about motivation, it must be mentioned—because without it there is no learning, no retention, no critical thinking. Motivation is the *sine qua non* of power thinking. Without it, all that has gone before, and all that is to come, is mere talk.

I have seen students in a university library sitting for hours with books opened in front of them, staring out of the window. No doubt these students tell their parents that they study for three or four hours each day. Well, they don't study; they put in time. They have no real desire to learn, and as a result they do not learn.

On the other hand, I have seen students "cramming" a course on the night before an examination. Their whole grade—perhaps their whole college career—depends on what they do the next morning. In three or four hours these students can sometimes learn almost the entire content of a sociology course or a history course. They can learn it because they *want* to, or because they *have* to. Cramming is not desirable because it leads to poor long-term retention. But it is amazingly effective in the short run, and it does illustrate the power of motivation.

Nothing more really needs to be said about how important motivation is in power thinking. If you want to do something badly enough, you will do it. That is sound psychology.

Building desire, or motivation, is in many ways like building a house. In building a house, you do not start with the interior finishing, then throw up the walls, and finally build a foundation. Instead, you start with the foundation—and it must be a solid foundation. The foundation of successful learning is motivation. After you have built the foundation—the desire to learn—you are ready to build the "walls"—the basic mental structure of an educated person: reading ability, clear observation, critical listening, and the rest.

If you put forth the necessary effort, you will gain power that you never dreamed possible. Not every step will be easy, however. Even Thomas A. Edison, one of the authentic American geniuses, said that "genius is one percent inspiration and 99 percent perspiration."

Like Edison, you, too, must work. The next eleven chapters of this book can be read in an evening, but a book's promise is not its fulfillment. Only if you resolve to acquire everything that is suggested here will you be on the way to greater mental power and greater success in life.

TEN TIPS FOR POWER THINKING

1. Remember that experience is the only teacher, that you cannot form sound conclusions until you have some basis for these conclusions.
2. Don't offer judgments unless you have factual, rather than simply emotional, ground for the judgments.

3. Pay close attention to the meanings of words. Remember that different words mean different things to different people.

4. Use words carefully, keeping in mind that they are effective instruments only if they are used with precision.

5. Never abandon your common sense, even if your experience seems to conflict with it.

6. Apply to new problems everything relevant that you have learned in the past.

7. Examine sources of information whose interpretations do not agree with your own.

8. Try to keep an open mind even when you disagree strongly with the other person's viewpoint.

9. Recognize glittering generalizations when you come across them. Remember that Cow_1 is not Cow_2.

10. Cultivate a desire to learn. Let no obstacle stand in the way of achieving this desire.

Chapter 2 ═══════════════

The Art of Accurate Observation

- Let's See
- Beware of Visual Tricks
- Notice Similarities
- Notice Differences
- Objective Observation
- Five Tips for Accurate Observation

"SEEING IS BELIEVING" IS A WITHERED adage that should be given a decent burial. Far too many of us "see" in much the same way as the fabled blind men who "saw" the elephant—part by part, with almost no realization of what we see. To form beliefs on the basis of such observations is sheer folly. To act on the basis of such "seeing" is sometimes disastrous.

The art of accurate observation, of truly *seeing*, is very nearly a lost art. Television, which has been called "the opiate of the masses," is partly to blame. We no longer see; we look or we watch. Yet accurate observation is one of the essential steps to power thinking, and it deserves to be revived. If your experience is to have meaning, you must be able to observe accurately and generalize from what you have seen.

Conversely, however, before you can learn *by* observing, you must learn *to* observe.

LET'S SEE

A college professor told me about a student who complimented him on his necktie at the beginning of class. Halfway through the class—which, incidentally, concerned the techniques of careful observation—the professor turned his back and asked members of the class to describe his tie. None could do it, not even the one who had complimented him on the tie. In fact, that student could not tell him the color of it.

Many such examples could easily be demonstrated, but the point is clear: You do not always see what you look at. If you doubt the truth of this statement, close your eyes and try to describe in detail the clothes you are wearing. Can you do it? Some people can, of course, but many more cannot. A few husbands, I am told, do not even know the color of their wives' eyes; but that situation surely must be unusual.

Take a quick look at the writing in these two triangles·

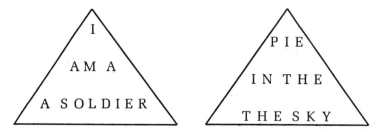

What did you read? Four out of five people looking at these triangles will say, "I am a soldier" and "Pie in the sky." But that is not what is printed within the triangles. Look again. "I am *a a* soldier" and "Pie in *the the* sky" are the actual statements. If you did not read them correctly the first time, you simply did not observe carefully. Instead, you saw what you expected to see—one of the most prevalent causes of inaccurate observation.

BEWARE OF VISUAL TRICKS

In a psychology class, a teacher held up a large playing card that was a *red* four of *spades*. (Spades, of course, are supposed to be black.) Then the teacher laid the card face down on the desk and asked the students to describe it. Twenty-seven out of twenty-eight called it either a *black* four of spades or a red four of *hearts*. Only one student actually saw the card for what it was: a visual trick.

If such visual tricks were restricted to psychology classrooms, you could laugh about the experiment and forget it. Unfortunately, similar visual tricks are played on you in business and industry, on television, and in books, magazines, and newspapers. Some of these tricks are consciously planned to mislead you, as for example a movie advertisement that quotes a reviewer as having said, ". . .great. . .colossal," when the reviewer actually said. "This movie is a *great* waste of time and a *colossal* failure." Those ellipses (. . .) are the visual trick. You should notice them. You should know that they indicate omissions, in this case some very important omissions.

Some visual tricks are not necessarily meant to mislead you, but they can be dangerous nonetheless. When a company's annual report is printed on slick paper with four-color illustrations, you should still read the figures in the report. However impressive the report may be as a high-quality printing job—and however substantial the company may therefore appear—you had better make sure that sales and profits are still what they ought to be. A beautiful package can hide some pretty ugly facts. Only careful observation can make you aware of the truth.

To repeat, you see what you expect to see, or what you want to see, or what you think you should see. There is only one way to guard against being misled, and that is to observe consciously, carefully, and critically.

NOTICE SIMILARITIES

When you look at something, you should do so with an open mind, but not with a vacant mind. Let's say you are a salesperson who has been asked to evaluate the sales potential of a new product your company is introducing. From the preceding chapter, you will remember that any such evaluation will proceed from partial ignorance. However, you can lessen that ignorance substantially by making some careful observations. You can look at the product and compare it with previous products or the products of competing companies. Does the past experience of your own or competing companies indicate that buyers are looking for something approximately like this? Are there similarities in design, size, color, price, and so on? If so, it may be safe to conclude that there will be some similarity in sales potential. At any rate, you should not disregard the similarities between the new product and older ones. These similarities can be extremely significant, for people's needs and wants do not change overnight.

People who notice similarities have a tremendously valuable tool for repeating past successes, their own or someone else's. It has been said that the musical scores in Rodgers and Hammerstein musicals all follow a certain pattern. The implication is that Rodgers and Hammerstein carefully analyzed *Oklahoma*, their first hit, as a guide to future productions. "Why did *Oklahoma* succeed?" they asked. "What blend of ingredients made it popular?" "Would a similar, but not precisely the same, blend produce another hit?" Their answer to the last question was that it might—and it certainly did. Thus, it is possible to "match" songs from say, *Oklahoma, South Pacific,* and *The King and I* and to see the successful pattern, or formula, within which Rodgers and Hammerstein worked. These men were masters at observing similarities and then putting them to use. You should acquire the same habit.

NOTICE DIFFERENCES

If you were trying to estimate the sales potential of a product, you would look not only for significant similarities (desirable ones) but also for significant *differences* (also desirable ones). The desirable differences are often called "gimmicks," though the word *gimmicks* has undeservedly offensive connations. The difference, or gimmick, may be important or it may be trivial. If it is important, it can lead to fantastic sales success and widespread acceptance. Witness the success of car telephones, microwave ovens, and fax machines.

The importance of noticing similarities and differences can hardly be overestimated. Most progress—personal, professional, and societal—is based on careful observation. You can't "make a better mousetrap" unless you know what is wrong (and what is right) with all the current mousetraps.

OBJECTIVE OBSERVATION

No matter how accurately you observe and how brilliantly you draw conclusions from your observations, you will not be entirely objective. This is an important point to remember, because most people seem to think that complete objectivity is easily attainable. Nothing could be more untrue, for complete objectivity is beyond the reach of anyone. A *New York Times* reporter is not wholly objective, nor is a justice of the Supreme Court, nor a research chemist, nor a teacher, nor a sales manager, nor a saint.

A power thinker can only *approach* objectivity; never perfectly achieve it. There are obvious reasons for this. When you observe, you observe with all your being and all your senses. What you are, what you have been, and what you hope to be—all of these inevitably color your observations.

The moral is this: You can observe accurately only within your limitations—and *everyone* has certain limitations. These limitations include your hopes, your fears, your likes, and your dislikes. It is impossible to discount such factors, for they are built into your mind and heart.

What does this mean in terms of power thinking? It means (1) that you should recognize your own prejudices and, insofar as possible, take them into account when reaching conclusions or making decisions, and (2) that you should recognize the motives, prejudices, and limitations of the people with whom you come into contact. You can, and must, take these limitations into account if you are to become a power thinker.

To illustrate one failure of objectivity: I know a former high school English teacher who refused to have his students study grammar, because, he said, "It's a useless subject." He was fired after one year, and rightly so, because his conclusion about English grammar was an emotional one entirely. He overlooked the fact that thousands of school administrators have for years considered English grammar a necessary subject, and more important, alas, he ignored the fact that the state in which he taught demanded the teaching of grammar. As he later confided to me, this teacher *did* think that English grammar was necessary—but he didn't like the subject, he didn't know it well, and he didn't feel competent to teach it. Instead of admitting this and doing something about it, he constructed a wild rationalization, to wit, that the subject ought not to be taught, by him or presumably by anyone else.

An accurate observer would have taken her emotions into account. She would have realized that even a minimum of objectivity indicated, under the circumstances, the necessity of teaching English grammar.

In addition to recognizing your own limitations when it comes to observing and drawing sensible conclusions, you should recognize the limitations of other people in this respect. A true Marxist, for instance, cannot see the fallacies of dialectical materialism, even when these fallacies stand in concrete form before his very eyes. "No doubt," said a friend of mine, "there are some visitors to the United States who think that New York City is a papier-mâché miracle, thrown up on a few hours notice especially for their visit. And all these cars! No doubt driven from every point in the country expressly to make an impression on the foreign visitors. ' An exaggeration, of course, but there are a great many people who literally will not credit their own eyes and ears if observations conflict with prejudices or predilections. .

Objective observation—that is, *absolutely* objective—is impossible. But a power thinker will credit her eyes and ears even if the evidence they provide seems to conflict with her beliefs. Power thinking requires at least an approach to objectivity.

FIVE TIPS FOR ACCURATE OBSERVATION

1. Recognize the difference between *looking* and *seeing*. To see is to notice details, to interpret, to draw conclusions.

2. Don't be misled by "seeing" only what you expect to see. You must train yourself to see what actually exists, not just what you think ought to exist.

3. Be alert to visual tricks that can make you misinterpret what you see—or think you see.

4. Notice similarities and differences in the things you observe. Accurate observers make good use of what they see.

5. Try to be as objective as possible in your observations, but recognize that complete objectivity cannot be attained by you or anyone else.

Chapter 3

Dynamics of Effective Listening

- The Importance of Listening Well
- Requirements for Effective Listening
- You Must Be an Active Listener
- Is the Speaker an Expert?
- Listen Carefully to What Is Said
- Don't Ignore the Big Words
- Determine the Speaker's Motive
- Don't React Too Fast
- Encouraging the Nonspeaker
- Tall Tales, Long Stories, and Short Tempers
- Remain Calm!
- Ten Tips for Effective Listening

$\mathbf{Y}$OU HAVE BEEN HEARING ABOUT the "three Rs" almost since you were old enough to walk. But have you ever heard about the "one L"? Probably not, although it is something psychologists and professional educators are giving more attention to every day. The "one L" is *listening.*

Perhaps you think that anyone can listen well and that the skill requires no practice. If so, you are wrong. Examples of poor listening and even nonlistening are abundant. The classic example is Orson Welles's radio broadcast of *The War of the Worlds;* fully one million people missed three announcements about the fictional nature of the program, overlooked the general incredibility of the broadcast, and were completely convinced that flame-spitting Martians had just landed near Princeton, New Jersey, and were about to ravage the land. Not one of these one million people was actually listening.

THE IMPORTANCE OF LISTENING WELL

The importance of effective listening can hardly be overstated. Although the mythical Martian nonsense of Orson Welles occurs only once in a lifetime, other less spectacular listening situations occur every day.

It is obvious that a worker who completely ignores what his boss is saying will soon be out on the street. But what about the one who customarily hears part—but *only* part—of what his boss is saying? He is pretty likely to make it to the street, too, though it may take a little longer.

The effective listener, on the other hand, has a tremendous advantage on any kind of job. She hears what is being said, and she acts on it. She evaluates what is being said, and she profits by it. She has the reputation of being sharper than her fellow workers—and she is.

Of course, all people listen to some extent. Yet few people listen well; few people hear everything that is said. Few people try to "read between the lines" when they are listening. These people do not realize that failure to listen properly is both a deterrent to effective learning and a roadblock to personal success.

Listening, in fact, is considered to be just as important in the learning process as reading. For one thing, research has shown that we listen three times as much as we read. Listening is important and it is also interesting. Many people find it far more enjoyable than reading.

Indeed, there are sound reasons for learning how to listen, and listen well.

REQUIREMENTS FOR EFFECTIVE LISTENING

Listening is not really a simple matter. Contrary to popular opinion, it requires much more than just keeping one's mouth shut. Everyone in high school or college has seen students who stare raptly at the teacher for a full period, apparently wide-awake, seeming to digest every word, every nuance. These same students, judging by tests or oral questions, seem to have learned nothing and heard not a word.

What, then, does effective listening require? It requires active, aggressive participation in the speaker's thought. It demands genuine concentration, not faked attention.

If you are going to be a good listener, you must be able to appraise the speaker as to expertness, and, in doing so, determine how much weight should be given to the speaker's words. You must grasp the main idea. In addition, you must pay attention to the words used, noticing whether they are concrete, abstract, meaningless, or "loaded."

You must also know whether the speaker is seeking the truth or merely trying to push a pet theory. You cannot make the mistake of reacting too fast or of drawing conclusions too quickly.

All in all, effective listening is a real challenge.

YOU MUST BE AN ACTIVE LISTENER

Listening cannot be passive. As Dr. Dominick A. Barbara points out in his book *The Art of Listening* (Springfield, IL: Charles C. Thomas, 1974), mutual understanding requires *shared* meanings. If you are not willing to put forth real effort as a listener, you will not be able to share the speaker's meaning. You will not be able to share his or her thought.

Most poor listening results because listeners do not even try to share the speaker's thought. They aren't interested enough. They find the subject dull. But as G. K. Chesterton once said, "There is no such thing as an uninteresting subject; there are only uninterested people."

To be an effective listener, you must be interested in what is being said. This means you must abandon your prejudices about certain subjects, then make a special effort to listen, and listen aggressively, when these "uninteresting" subjects are discussed. Look for something of real value *to you* in all speeches and discussions. You will usually find it. Also, ask questions. Pretend you are interested—and soon you will be.

IS THE SPEAKER AN EXPERT?

When Albert Einstein talked about physics, even the President of the United States listened. But when he talked about politics, the seediest ward heeler in town was likely to walk away. Why? Because Einstein was an expert in physics; he knew what he was talking about. In politics, however, he was no more knowledgeable than the next person; in fact, many thought he was a bit duller than the average citizen.

Everyone has areas of competence and areas of ignorance. When a listener makes the mistake of assuming that a person who knows the ins and outs of the stock market also knows how to pick the ponies at Aqueduct, he is flirting with disaster. Yet this mistake is made very day. Otherwise sane people accept medical advice from their favorite mechanic and automotive tips from the family doctor. Don't you do it.

Very well, you say. But how does one decide whether the speaker is an expert? In most cases you don't have to decide, for it is already quite clearly established. An M.D. is presumed to know something about medicine. An auto mechanic is supposed to know something about your car's engine. A nuclear physicist should know quite a bit about the nature of atoms. Listen to these people *speaking on their own subjects* and you will not waste your time.

LISTEN CAREFULLY TO WHAT IS SAID

In addition to being an active participant and judging the expertness of the speaker, you must listen carefully to what is said.

Just listen carefully. . .that sounds like an easy rule, doesn't it? But how many people do you know who listen with their hearts instead of their minds? Too many people make the error of assuming that eloquence equals intelligence and that a smooth style of delivery guarantees truthfulness of content.

Aristotle said, "Persuasion may come through the hearers when the speech stirs their emotions." Hitler operated on that principle. So do many politicians, fast-talking used-car salespeople and others of that breed. Their words may be utter nonsense, but their way of saying them convinces the unwary.

Take the amazing case of Lozier, the persuasive carpenter. Back in 1824, this wizened little fellow convinced his Manhattan neighbors that the Battery section of Manhattan Island was sagging under the weight of too many buildings. He had talked with Mayor Stephen Allen, he said, and persuaded him there was imminent danger of the island's breaking in half because of the excess weight. What could be done, the major wanted to know. Lozier had an ingenious answer. Saw Manhattan Island off at Kingsbridge at the northern end, float it into the harbor, turn it around, float it back, and anchor the Battery section to the mainland. Lozier told his neighbors he had been commissioned by Mayor Allen to supervise the job. It would be quite a task, said Lozier. The saws would have to be 100 feet long with teeth three feet high. Two dozen oars would be needed, each oar 250 feet long, and huge oarlocks would have to be placed on both sides of Manhattan Island.

All this is ridiculous, you say. True. But Lozier, who accepted job applications for the great work, signed up over 300 of his gullible neighbors as "sawers" and "rowers."

Remember—a speaker may have a tongue of silver, but a

heart and brain of tin. Unless you judge a speaker by what is actually said rather than by the manner of delivery, you will fall victim to a good many smooth-talking charlatans. You are not likely to agree to saw off Manhattan Island, or even to buy the Brooklyn Bridge, but you may do things almost as foolish.

An effective listener hears precisely *what* is being said. He or she pays much less attention to the *way* it is being said.

DON'T IGNORE THE BIG WORDS

Big words are stumbling blocks for many listeners, yet they cannot be ignored without serious loss of comprehension.

John Kenneth Galbraith, U. S. Ambassador to India in the Kennedy administration, often used big words. He made the following observation in a speech at Annamalai University:

> It is not essential that the criticism which wins change be valid. Much of it has a ritual quality. Our trade unions win increases in pay only after appearing to affirm the classic prediction of Marx that workers under capitalism undergo progressive immiserization.

Do you know what the word *immiserization* means? You won't find it in any standard desk dictionary, so you should not be embarrassed if you can't give an exact definition. However, unless you have an inkling of what it means, you do not have a clear picture of what Mr. Galbraith said.

This is a dilemma all listeners face. Many of them respond by ignoring the big words completely, and by doing so they stamp themselves as poor listeners. Surely Mr. Galbraith meant something with that word *immiserization*. He wasn't simply trying to confuse the assembled group.

A good listener will make every effort to understand what is being said. Usually the big words will not come in such a deluge that you will be drowned under them. Only once in a while will a word like *immiserization* occur. When it does, you should try to understand what it means. The context will help. In this case, Mr. Galbraith was speaking of Karl Marx's philosophy. If you know that philosophy, you have a clue. Often, too, the root of the word will help. In this case it seems obvious the big word comes from the common little word *misery*. So apparently, Mr. Galbraith was saying that American labor unions demand pay increases on the grounds that their members are getting poorer and more miserable all the time. That's a very rough translation, of course, but it does convey the idea—which, as a listener, is what you are basically seeking.

It goes without saying that a strong vocabulary is a powerful tool for listening. You simply will not have enough time to puzzle out the meaning of very many words in a speech or conversation.

In a person-to-person talk, of course, you can and should ask for definitions of unfamiliar words. Any good speaker will rephrase a statement for you. If she can't rephrase it sensibly, there is a possibility she doesn't really know what she is trying to say any more than you do.

Meaningless jargon is a common and cancerous disease of many occupational groups. Long words and involved sentences *can* add up to great thought—but they can also add up to no thought at all. Sometimes a person with a large or technical vocabulary will use it solely to make an impression on his listeners. If this is the case, it's a good idea to bring the speaker down to earth.

In no case should you merely forget about the big words. As an effective listener, you must either find out what they mean or else establish beyond a doubt that they mean nothing. Otherwise, you will be at the mercy of every speaker with a large or technical vocabulary.

DETERMINE THE SPEAKER'S MOTIVE

If a used car salesman lauds the 1985 Chrysler (which he just happens to have on his lot) as the best automobile ever vouchsafed to man, you will quickly become a critical listener. You will conclude in all likelihood that he wants to sell it to you—regardless of its merits.

You should be just as careful when listening to speakers whose motives are not so apparent. Many people are brilliantly persuasive when selling a product or an idea. They present their thoughts well, with little or no hint of their real intent. But unless you are able to isolate their motive from their words, you will not be an effective listener.

How can you tell a speaker's motive? Ask yourself these questions:

- Does the speaker stand to gain financially or occupationally by converting you to his viewpoint?
- Will the speaker gain status by having her views accepted?
- Can the speaker gain some future advantage with his present words?
- Is the speaker using words to rid herself of frustrations?

Once you know the answer to these questions, you should have a fairly clear picture of why the speaker is talking. That "why" is extremely important. Unless you know the speaker's objective, your listening will lack effectiveness. Although you will hear the speaker's words, you will not be able to follow her spoken (or unspoken) thoughts. Your answer to the question, "What did the speaker say?" can be little better than Hamlet's answer to Polonius, "Words, words, words."

DON'T REACT TOO FAST

Here are some important words of caution:

Don't react too fast to what the speaker is saying.

Don't draw conclusions too quickly.

Don't try to evaluate what is being said until you understand it fully.

These simple rules are often violated. In the heat of discussion, it is all too easy to decide that the speaker has nothing important to say before you really know whether she does or not. You may make hasty, unreasonable efforts to contradict her.

Consider Patrick Henry's famous speech to the Virginia House of Burgesses:

Tarquin and Caesar each had his Brutus, Charles the First his Cromwell, and George the Third—["Treason!" cried the Speaker]—*may profit by their example.* If this be treason, make the most of it.

The Speaker of the House of Burgesses had jumped to conclusions. He apparently thought Patrick Henry was about to suggest the assassination of King George III. Thus, he was not a good listener, for good listening requires forbearance.

Even though a speaker's first remarks may seem open to criticism, you should not discount or discredit them too soon. It may be that the speaker really does have something worthwhile to say. If not, it can hardly hurt you to wait a bit before starting an argument or walking out or falling asleep.

ENCOURAGING THE NONSPEAKER

First of all, why bother to encourage the nonspeaker? A parable may answer the question.

The greatest military genius of all time, according to Mark Twain, was not Caesar or Napoleon, but a "bricklayer from somewhere back of Boston." His name was Absalom Jones. Of course, no one ever learned of Jones's great gift (until he reached heaven) because poor Absalom never had a chance to put his genius to work. Missing both thumbs and two front teeth, he was turned down by an ignorant recruiting sergeant.

So it is with the nonspeaker. She may have a world of wisdom to impart, but unless she can be made to speak, no one is going to get a chance to listen to her. No one is going to learn much from her.

How, then, can a nonspeaker be encouraged to say something? Naturally the easiest way is to ask her outright: "What do you think of that last statement, Ms. Saylittle?" This may be an effective technique in some cases, but it does have two defects. Its intent is so obvious that it may embarrass the nonspeaker unless used very early in the discussion. Also, it is unlikely to encourage the nonspeaker to say more than a few words.

A nonspeaker lacks self-confidence. Since this is so, a good way to get her talking is to build up her ego: "You know, fellow listeners, Ms. Saylittle here knows more about widgets than all the rest of us put together. I believe she was one of the developers of the microwidget." Such a remark almost forces the nonspeaker to say something, if only to enter a modest denial of her competence. And this denial, if you have your facts right, will not be accepted by the other listeners. Thus, the nonspeaker will be required to participate in the discussion.

Another way to snare the nonspeaker is to make a remark, preferably a somewhat controversial one, that hits her right in her area of competence. For instance, if the nonspeaker is an avid Civil War buff from Georgia, a comment like, "I've heard it said that General Sherman contributed more to the science of warfare than General Lee," would have a good chance of drawing some reply from her. Few people can resist the temptation to speak about subjects they know extremely well, or those on which they have strong feelings.

Often a nonspeaker making her first contribution will be interrupted by a more aggressive person, especially if the discussion is heated. In such a case, it is a good idea to demand that the nonspeaker be heard. If the nonspeaker has started to say something and has been interrupted, make it a point either to stop the interrupter immediately or else come back to the nonspeaker as soon as the interrupter has finished speaking. Otherwise, the nonspeaker may give up before even having a chance to begin.

Whenever a nonspeaker has finished making her first contribution to a discussion, compliment her on it. Of course, if she has made a complete fool of herself—which is rare for the nonspeaker—don't insist on following suit by praising her foolishness. But an honest compliment, sincerely given, will go far toward persuading her to speak again.

TALL TALES, LONG STORIES, AND SHORT TEMPERS

The exact opposite of the nonspeaker is the know-it-all and say-it-all character familiar to everyone. With such a person, speaking is a disease. He needs therapy, and you must be able to give it to him if the discussion is not to become a soliloquy.

Stopping the compulsive talker demands nerve. You, the listener, must be willing to risk antagonizing him or you can accomplish nothing. Given the necessary courage, you should be able to stop the haranguer in one of these ways:

1. *Ignore him.* Ask questions of other members of the group. If the haranguer tries to interrupt other speakers,

pay no attention to him; instead, concentrate on what the interrupted speaker is saying. If necessary, you should consider making a remark such as this to the interrupted speaker: "Pardon me, would you repeat that last sentence. There seems to be some static in the air, and I'm having a hard time hearing you." This should be said with a smile.

2. *Tell the haranguer to get to the point.* You can do this more gently with a question than with a direct statement. Try one of the following:

   a. "What do you conclude from all this, Mr. Neverstop?"

   b. "I take it, Mr. Neverstop, you think. . ." and draw the apparent conclusion yourself. This requires a qualified "yes" or "no" from him, and allows you to ask another person to comment on the answer.

   c. "Yes, but what, if anything, are you trying to prove, Mr. Neverstop?" This is not so gentle, but the haranguer is not usually a thin-skinned type.

3. *Interrupt the haranguer with a positive, contradictory statement and ask another member of the group to comment on it.* For instance, "You're wrong there, Mr. Neverstop. . .Wouldn't you say so, Ms. Fellowsufferer?" A remark like this makes it practically impossible for the haranguer to continue. He cannot, with good grace, ignore both you *and* Ms. Fellowsufferer.

Once you have learned how to handle the haranguer, you should have little trouble with his first cousin, the teller of tall tales. Now, many speakers use gross exaggeration as a device to enliven their speech. These people are harmless at worst and fascinating at best. But unfortunately there is one kind of tall-tale teller who must be described as a liar. She can be treated in much the same way as the haranguer. If she is particularly notorious, however, you may wish to summon your courage and give her a straightforward challenge: "I don't believe you." Everyone, including the liar, will respect you for it.

REMAIN CALM

Both haranguers and tellers of tall tales sometimes cause a group discussion to get out of hand. This can result in short tempers among all members of the group. Also, as you well know, there are certain subjects that can lead to harsh words; politics and religion are the best known. When a discussion seems on the verge of chaos because of short tempers, a listener who maintains composure and a sense of humor is the group's last hope to save the day.

TEN TIPS FOR EFFECTIVE LISTENING

1. Don't say a subject is uninteresting, for all subjects are interesting. There are, however, uninterested listeners.
2. Gauge the speaker's expertise on the subject under discussion. Listen carefully to the person who knows what he or she is talking about.
3. Don't equate eloquence with intelligence. A very poor speaker may say a great deal, while a brilliant speaker may say nothing.
4. Make every effort to understand the big words used by a speaker. Demand understandable English of people addicted to jargon.
5. Require concrete statements in place of emotion-laden cliches.
6. Determine the speaker's motive before you try to evaluate the message.
7. Don't draw conclusions too quickly. Give the speaker a chance to make his point before trying to contradict it. Evaluate only when comprehension is complete.
8. Learn how to get the nonspeaker into a group discussion.
9. Use every possible method to silence the haranguer and teller of tall tales.
10. Retain your composure and sense of humor. Effective listening demands real effort, and such effort is impossible in an atmosphere highly charged with emotion.

Chapter 4

How to Increase Your Reading Efficiency

- Dynamics of Rapid Reading
- Selecting What to Read
- Read More, Speed More
- What Is Holding You Back?
- Try to Read Faster
- Phrase-Reading vs. Word-Reading
- Watch for the Signposts
- The Whys and Hows of Intelligent Skimming
- Reading for the Main Idea
- How to Increase Your Comprehension
- Budget Your Reading Time
- Concentrate, Concentrate, Concentrate
- Ten Tips for Increased Reading Efficiency

Most people would admit to a desire to read more than they do now. And there is one excellent way to make this wish become a reality. Learn to read faster! Unquestionably you can do this, and it is well worth the effort.

Consider this fact: A really outstanding reader could race through *Mental Dynamics*, cover-to-cover, with full comprehension, in less than two hours. By contrast, the average reader will take nearly six hours to finish the book. Which means, of course, that an extremely efficient reader can cover, day in and day out, three times as much material as the average reader *in the same length of time*. This startling fact helps account for the growth of interest in speed reading.

Now, you are not likely to be able to increase your own reading speed threefold, regardless of what some exponents of speed reading may say. But no matter how fast or slowly you read, you can almost certainly increase your speed by 20 percent to 100 percent. This has been proved time and time again by reading institutes, reading clinics, and reading laboratories throughout the country. The techniques of speed reading are easy to learn. The results are amazing, and the benefits are obvious.

So, here we go. . .

DYNAMICS OF RAPID READING

Many people do very little reading. Many others read unselectively. The first essential step in any rapid reading program is (a) to make up your mind to read more, and (b) to choose what you do read very carefully. The next step is to make a conscious effort to read faster. These two steps alone are likely to help you increase your reading efficiency, even if you do little else.

Really getting started on the program, however, requires that you learn how to read whole phrases at a glance, not just single words. You must train yourself to see in a flash the written material you formerly lingered over. You must learn the art of sensible skimming and the technique of reading for main ideas rather than for isolated facts.

As you work on your personal speed-reading program, you will budget your reading time; you will strive to improve your comprehension; and, above all, you will concentrate on what you read.

That in a nutshell is all there is to speed reading. Of course, this makes it sound a little easier than it actually is, because every step in the program demands hard work and a great deal of serious reading.

Let's look at each step in more detail.

SELECTING WHAT TO READ

Ann Frazier is a young mechanical engineer. Her job requires that she read technical magazines, surveys, and reports for at least two hours of every working day. In addition to this required reading, she regularly scans a morning tabloid newspaper but, commuting by subway from Brooklyn Heights to lower Manhattan, she seldom gets past the front page, the entertainment page, and the comics. She subscribes to two women's magazines and she reads about five books a year, mostly popular fiction.

Ann's reading habits are not unusual. In fact, they are quite average. And, unfortunately, Ann is not a well-informed person. She cannot carry on a stimulating conversation with her equally intelligent co-workers who, in contrast, read widely. She is undoubtedly hurting her chances for advancement, for no company wants dull, uninformed executives. Yet Ann was regarded as a superior student in both high school and college and is a first-rate engineer.

Ann Frazier reads at the rate of 280 words a minute, a little above the national average. She could probably double that reading speed if she were to put her mind to it. But the big question is this: What good would it do her?

Ann could not and should not read technical material much faster than she does now. Technical material is not the kind of reading that lends itself to rapid reading. Of course, she could become a more accomplished skimmer, as will be shown later, but that in itself would be of only moderate value to her.

She could read twice as much in the morning newspaper as she does now. She could presumably dash through four picture magazines a month and she could double her intake of detective fiction. These things she could do in the same amount of time she now spends reading. But would she have gained anything? Not much, it would seem. She would still be ill-informed and only superficially aware of what reading could do for her, and is doing for her fellow workers.

What Ann needs to do right now is alter her reading habits, not double her reading speed. She needs to challenge herself with tougher, more provocative, deeper, and more varied reading fare. *Then*, if she doubles her reading speed, she will truly profit by it.

Let's say Ann decides to read the *New York Times* each day, concentrating on the front page articles and the editorial page; to read the Sunday *Times*, paying special attention to the "News of the Week in Review," the Magazine section, and the Book Review section. Let's say (rather arbitrarily) that she chooses two new magazines, *U. S. News and World Report* and *Harper's* and selects five solid books to read next year: one modern novel, one classic (perhaps *Huckleberry Finn*, which she has never read), one book of popular history, one book about contemporary politics, and one book on popular science.

This may not be an ideal reading program—for it is too limited—but it is clearly superior to her present one. And even if Ann continues to read at only 280 words a minute, she is going to be much better informed than she is now. If, after changing her reading habits, she decides to work on increasing her reading rate, she will of course be making a wise move.

The point is this: There is no reason whatever to double one's reading speed if it merely means that one is going to read twice as much trivia. Two times nothing is still nothing.

READ MORE, SPEED MORE

Let's say you have decided, if necessary, to improve the quality of your daily reading, and now you want to step up the pace of your reading. How do you go about doing it? Well, for one thing, you read more.

Consider this fact. If you are presently reading about 20 books a year, you are probably reading faster than the person who reads only five. Why? Because you are a more experienced reader and you get more enjoyment out of reading. You have had more *practice* in reading and you are more *interested* in reading.

Practice and interest are just as essential to success in reading as they are to success in any other activity. The tennis player who practices the game and enjoys playing it will eventually have a faster serve and a faster volley than the court dilettante who can take the game or leave it alone. The stenographer who types eight hours a day will be faster, as a rule, than the one who types only one hour.

Now, an avid reader will not make astounding weekend gains in reading speed without conscious effort to do so. Nor will a person who normally reads five books a year become a speed demon in one year just because he or she reads twenty. But the person who reads 20 books year in and year out will, through sheer experience, become a more competent and somewhat faster reader than the one who forever reads five.

"Yes," you say, "but I want to increase my reading speed now—not sometime in the next 30 years." All right, you can. but you may still have to make up your mind to read more than you do at present. Practice is the key to improvement in almost every endeavor, and speed reading is no exception. The only kind of practice there is for speed reading is reading, reading, and more reading. Thus, if you are a once-in-a-blue-moon reader, you will simply have to become a once-a-night reader. One quarter of an hour a day is the very least you can devote to your reading program if you expect to see lasting improvement. One full hour is far better.

To sum up: Before you begin to work on speed reading per se, you should make three important resolutions:

- To read genuinely worthwhile newspapers, magazines, and books.
- To read more in the future than you have been reading in the past.

• To spend at least 15 minutes every day of the year on a planned reading program.

WHAT IS HOLDING YOU BACK?

Assuming that you have decided to raise the quality and quantity of your reading, the first step toward improving your reading efficiency is to break yourself of any bad physical habits you may have developed. Here is a checklist of poor but common reading habits that ought to be broken:

The Habit	The Remedy
1. Sounding out words in silent reading.	Stop all lip movement. Check yourself from time to time in order to make sure you are not vocalizing. Chewing gum while you read may help break this habit.
2. Pointing to words or to lines with your fingers.	Hold the book, magazine, or newspaper with both hands. This will keep your fingers occupied and prevent you from pointing.
3. Rereading words, phrases, or whole sentences in relatively simple, nontechnical material.	Concentrate! Refuse yourself the luxury of rereading. Even if you are quite sure you have missed something of importance, forget it for the time being. Keep going. If necessary, use a plain white card to cover up lines you have read.
4. Moving your head from side to side.	Make certain you are reading only with your eyes. If necessary, hold your chin firmly in your hand to help break this habit.

TRY TO READ FASTER

There are many techniques for increasing your reading speed and at least one of them is absurdly easy—*try* to read faster.

Norman Lewis, author of *How to Read Better and Faster*, 4th edition (New York: Harper & Row, 1978), points out that merely trying to read faster can often bring striking gains in reading speed.

By way of proof, Mr. Lewis tells about a remarkable experiment he used to conduct with beginning students in his Adult Reading Laboratory. He would ask these students to read a short article at their normal reading pace. He would ask them to pretend they were at home in their favorite easy chair and not being tested at all. He would then time them on this selection.

Then Mr. Lewis would have them read a second, similar article, telling them to push through the article at a consciously faster rate. On the second selection, the students were not to sacrifice comprehension for speed, but were to concentrate harder and try to read more purposely. Once again the students were timed.

The results were amazing. Most students showed immediate reading rate improvements of from 20 to 50 percent.

You can do the same thing. Sounds impossible? Make the following test and prove it to yourself. When you come to the section in this chapter entitled The Whys and Hows of Intelligent Skimming, read it at your normal rate. Settle back in your chair, relax, and go through the section at the same speed you have been using on the others. Make no effort to go faster, but, at the same time, don't stop of a coffee break in the middle. Proceed at your usual rate. Time yourself on the section, then check your present reading rate in the Appendix, page 177. Write this word-per-minute rate in the space provided.

When you read the next section after this "normal speed" one—Reading for the Main Idea—time yourself again and *try to read as fast as you possible can without sacrificing comprehension*. Don't dawdle. Don't let your mind wander. Push right through to the end. Then check your new reading rate in Appendix A. The chances are at least ten to one it will be somewhat better than it was before.

The lesson is obvious. Most of us are lazy readers. We do not read as fast *any* of the time we could be reading *all* the time. The remedy for the fault is also clear. Try to read faster all the time—whenever you pick up a newspaper, book, or magazine—and not just when you are testing yourself for speed. You will be amazed at the improvement in your reading efficiency.

PHRASE READING VERSUS WORD READING

Once you have determined to *try* to read faster, you have established a firm base for all the remaining steps in a speed reading program.

You will, for example, automatically begin forcing yourself to read longer groups of words at a single glance, not just one word, two words, or three words at a time. There is nothing difficult about this. All efficient readers do it.

Here is a graphic illustration of the eye pauses made by slow and fast readers:

Slow: Some/poor/readers/actually/stop,/look,/and think/af-
            ter/nearly/every/word.

Fast: Some poor readers/actually stop, look, and think/
            after nearly every word.

It is impossible, of course, to read very fast if you pause after every word. It is also impossible to read with a high degree of comprehension if you do this. Each word is merely part of a whole thought, and to understand written material well you must *read for the thought*, not for the individual words. The only way you can grasp thought units is by reading entire phrases (instead of words) at a single glance.

You may not be reading this book word-by-word, for most intelligent adults have already learned to read by phrases—or, more accurately, by ideas or meaningful word groups. However, your thought units in reading may be shorter (two or three words) than they could or should be (four, five, or six words). By increasing the length of these units, you can increase your reading speed substantially.

Note that when you try to read faster, you are unconsciously trying to get rid of unnecessary pauses in your reading. By consciously trying to do it, you can add valuable words-per-minute to your reading rate.

WATCH FOR THE SIGNPOSTS

As you strive to increase the number of words you can see and understand at a single glance, you should pay close attention to words or phrases which tell in a split second whether there is going to be an abrupt change in the author's trend of thought, or whether, on the contrary, the writer is merely going to add more details to what has already been said.

Some of the common "turnabout signals" are these: *but, despite, on the contrary, however, nonetheless, yet,* and *rather.* As soon as the reader sees these words, she will know instantaneously that the author is about to introduce a thought in opposition to the one she has just stated.

The other kind of direction words are ones the author uses to tell the reader that ideas similar to the preceding ones are going to be discussed. Some common examples are *and, moreover, furthermore, also, likewise, thus, therefore, consequently,* and *accordingly.* As soon as the reader sees these words, he knows there is not going to be an abrupt change in the author's trend of thought.

All readers, if they wish to attain maximum efficiency, must be able to spot these direction words quickly and unfailingly, and take appropriate cues from them.

THE WHYS AND HOWS OF INTELLIGENT SKIMMING*

Skimming is both a technique of speed reading and a process of selection and elimination. A reader does not skim for total meaning. Instead, she skims to determine what needs to be read thoroughly for total meaning.

Skimming, as Webster puts it, is "to read superficially and rapidly for the main ideas." Of course, there is a great deal of material that requires nothing more than skimming. A busi-

---

*Time yourself on this section in order to determine your best present reading rate. See page 44. The key to reading rates will be found in the Appendix.

nessperson's correspondence, for instance, contains some letters that are vital and some that are trivial. Skimming tells the businessperson which letters demand careful and immediate attention and which do not. It allows her to devote attention to letters which must be read carefully and answered promptly.

Skimming is a commonplace technique among readers of magazines and newspapers. No one settles back with a morning newspaper and reads it, article by article, from front to back. Nor do most people read every article and story in their favorite magazines.

Thus, skimming is a skill that most people have already developed to some extent. But what sets a competent skimmer apart from a poor skimmer, and how does one become versed in the proper methods of skimming? Here are some useful tips:

1. Know exactly what information you are looking for, what information you need. Otherwise your skimming will be pointless.

2. Always look at the table of contents of a nonfiction book. This will give you a far better picture of the whole book than you can get by simply leafing through it.

3. Don't overlook prefaces, forewords, tables of illustrations, and tables of graphs in nonfiction books. All such front matter, coupled with the table of contents, can provide you with valuable book "previews."

4. If you are looking for a specific item of information in a book, check the index. This may seem like a self-evident point, but librarians claim that many people seem to look upon indexes as mere decorative appendages to books.

5. Read only summaries of chapters if you want to get the gist of a book. Many textbooks have all essential information neatly summarized at the beginning or end of chapters.

6. Skip the parts of books and articles that do not contain material you need or want. In this connection, you should remember that newspaper reporters are taught to put the most important facts first, then to include items of gradually diminishing significance. This is done

mainly for editorial reasons; it allows cutting the length of articles without rewriting them. However, the device also allows readers to get the basic facts from a newspaper article without reading the article all the way through.

7 Read only for main ideas; skip details. This is a most important skill in speed reading and deserves special discussion.

READING FOR THE MAIN IDEA*

Many people get bogged down in a morass of details when they read. In some cases, meticulous reading is necessary. No one would try to race through a legal document or a college textbook at 1000 words per minute. But most material does not require such careful reading, and if you habitually plod along more slowly than you should you may pick up isolated facts and overlook the author's main ideas.

Read for main ideas! Don't be like the law student I knew who could remember the factual details of all the cases he read but had no idea of what point of law was involved in them. After all, details are illustrative of main ideas, but they are not usually the substance of them.

How can you read for main ideas? One way is to learn how to recognize topic sentences. Most well-written paragraphs contain one important sentence that sums up the content of the entire paragraph. Often (but not always) the topic sentence will be the first sentence in the paragraph.

An efficient reader can usually spot topic sentences with little effort. However, it takes practice to develop the skill. If you have difficulty with topic sentences, you should practice identifying them in your daily reading. The editorial page of your favorite newspaper is a good place to begin.

Another way to read for main ideas is to notice article titles, chapter titles, and subheadings. Ask yourself what points should be covered in these articles, chapters, and subsections. Then see if

---

*Time yourself on this section in order to determine your normal reading rate. See page 44. The key to reading rates will be found in the Appendix.

they are. By using this question-and-answer technique, you will train yourself to look for main ideas in whatever you read.

HOW TO INCREASE YOUR COMPREHENSION

Some books and magazine articles on rapid reading seem to adopt a rather cavalier attitude toward comprehension. The authors imply that if a person increases his or her reading speed, comprehension will improve along with it. But this is not necessarily true. It is possible to try to read *too* fast and sacrifice comprehension in the process. To do so is simply ridiculous, for comprehension is the essence of reading. Unless you understand what you are reading, there is little point in reading at all.

An individual's reading speed, like his IQ or college degree, appears to be in danger of becoming a sort of status symbol. Some people in public life have been heard to boast of their phenomenal reading rates. In this connection, one is reminded of the story of the New York commuter who noticed that the distinguished-looking gentleman who sat next to her each morning on the train was finishing his *Times* crossword puzzle every day in ten minutes flat. Immensely impressed by the apparent brilliance of the man, our awed commuter one morning picked up the *Times* after the great man had left his seat. Sure enough, every space was filled in—but only with meaningless letters, not with words. The daily ten-minute ritual of completing the puzzle was nothing but an outlandish sham designed to impress a group of total strangers.

Speed reading, if it is not to become an outlandish sham, must be accompanied by genuine comprehension. Indeed, the whole purpose of speed reading is to allow you to get more reading done and consequently to get more out of your reading. This aim is defeated by a person's striving for impossibly high words-per-minute rates and pretending to have attained them.

We have touched on some of the ways in which reading comprehension can be increased, and these methods are worth repeating:

- Read rapidly for *ideas*. Don't creep along by sounding out words, pointing to words, or rereading words.

- Remember that every author is trying to say something. The sooner you discover the theme, the intent, the focal point of an author's work, the better your comprehension will be.

- Previewing what you read will increase your comprehension. Don't dismiss tables of contents, prefaces, and sub-headings as superfluous. If you know the overall scheme of a book or article before you begin reading, your understanding of it will be improved and made easier.

- Use a question-and-answer technique in your reading. As soon as you have finished a book, a chapter, or an article, ask yourself pertinent questions about its contents.

BUDGET YOUR READING TIME

It has been noted that you should plan to spend at least 15 minutes every day on a reading improvement program. Of course, if you can set aside half an hour or one full hour each day, so much the better. The period you reserve for reading should, if possible, be at approximately the same time every day. This will help you establish an unbreakable habit of reading.

In addition to this reading budget, you should set a time limit for yourself on most books. Once you reach an optimum reading rate on a particular kind of book, you should force yourself to achieve that rate each and every day. By setting this goal for yourself—a specified number of pages each day—you will soon read as naturally at full speed as you are now reading at half or three-quarter speed.

CONCENTRATE, CONCENTRATE, CONCENTRATE

How many times have you read paragraphs or even whole pages, only to come to the sudden realization that you have no idea of what you have been reading? Probably quite often. Lack of concentration is the occasional bane of all readers.

How can you improve your powers of concentration? The easiest and most obvious way is to get rid of all possible distractions when you read. If possible, you should have a quiet spot in your house or apartment reserved for the purpose of reading.

Try to eliminate mental distractions as well. Unless you can bury yourself in the author's thought rather than in your own, your reading efficiency is bound to suffer. When you sit down to read, make a firm resolution to achieve complete rapport with your author. This does not mean you should be an uncritical reader, but only that you should make every effort to follow the author's thought. You will not be able to do this if your mind is on the news of the day or the latest office gossip.

Some people find it helpful to close their eyes for about five or ten seconds every ten minutes or so when they are reading. They feel that resting their eyes in this manner allows them to concentrate effectively for longer periods of time. The same result can be achieved by looking away from the printed page every now and then. Both methods are worth trying.

Remember: You must concentrate if you want to comprehend.

TEN TIPS FOR INCREASED READING EFFICIENCY

1. Read at least 15 minutes every day, and select your reading material carefully.
2. Eliminate poor physical habits such as sounding the words in silent reading; pointing to words or lines; and rereading words, phrases, or sentences.
3. Make a conscious and continuous effort to increase your reading speed.
4. Learn to read by thought units rather than by individual words. You should take in between four and six words at a single glance.
5. Watch for the signposts in reading. One kind tells you there will be a change in the trend of thought, the other that more details will be added to the same thought.
6. Know exactly what information you are looking for when you read factual material, then practice the art of skimming in order to find it.

7. Read for main ideas. Don't get bogged down in a morass of details in everyday reading.

8. Don't sacrifice comprehension for speed. Make sure you understand what you are reading.

9. Budget your reading time and force yourself to read at optimum speed.

10. Concentrate on what you are reading. Get rid of distractions. Rest your eyes occasionally.

Chapter 5

Power Thinking Techniques for Everyday English

- The Terrible Ten
- Spotting Your Mistakes
- How to Choose the Right Word
- Lowering the Cliché Count
- Omitting Needless Words
- Singular Subject, Singular Verb Form
- The Split Infinitive
- Scotching the Mysterious "It"
- A Simple Rule for Apostrophes
- "Where Do I Put the Quotation Marks?"
- Like and As
- Some Words That Bear Watching
- Ten Tips for Mastering Everyday English

TAKE A CLOSE, CRITICAL LOOK at the letters or reports you have written recently. Are they clear? Are they concise? There is a better than even chance that they aren't. Far too much that passes for communication in business and social life is ambiguous, over-blown, or meaningless. Most people find it difficult to express themselves in writing.

Yet from the standpoint of personal advancement, the ability to write clearly and accurately is of real importance. People who cannot express themselves in writing may never even get an interview for the jobs they want. And on their present job—if any writing at all is required —they will throw promotional opportunities to the winds if unable to "talk" on paper. No amount of personal charm can overcome this handicap.

Recall, if you will, the business letters you have seen recently. What was the job status of those who wrote the most impressive ones? Undoubtedly it was high. It is almost axiomatic that the best letters in any company are written by the executives highest on the ladder. As one goes down in the hierarchy, the quality of letters drop correspondingly.

There are no dark secrets about good English, and it doesn't take a genius to write meaningful, straightforward, and grammatically correct letters. English can be taught, and supposedly it is taught in every high school in the United States. But the subject is an unpopular one. Many students hate it, slight it, even fail it. Later they discover their mistake, and a serious mistake it is. The ability to write readable English—like the ability to listen well and the ability to read rapidly—is essential to success on many jobs.

This chapter, pinpointing ten common pitfalls in written English, is intended as a once-over-lightly look at basic grammar and composition. Don't slight it, for adequate English can pay off in dollars and cents.

THE TERRIBLE TEN

Because so many errors can be made in writing, it is hard to pick the ten worst or the ten most common. However, from my talks with teachers and editors, and from an examination of books on the subject, it seems clear that the following must be included:

The first pitfall: Using inexact words, or what Mark Twain called "the almost right" words. This problem stems more often from laziness than from a poor vocabulary.

The second pitfall: Using hackneyed expressions instead of original ones. Laziness again. No one can avoid clichés all the time, but just avoiding them part of the time will add sparkle to your business and social writing.

The third pitfall: Using too many words. This is an occupational hazard of the learned professions. It is also a common fault in many of the unlearned ones.

The fourth pitfall: Using plural subjects with singular forms of verbs and vice versa.

The fifth pitfall: Using split infinitives. English teachers by the score have gone berserk over this problem. It's hardly that important, but you should at least be able to recognize a split infinitive when you see or use one.

The sixth pitfall: Using pronouns with ambiguous or nonexistent antecedents. This may be the most common error of all. It is certainly one of the most annoying to readers.

The seventh pitfall: Using apostrophes in the wr places, particularly with the tricky possessives.

The eighth pitfall: Using quotation marks incorrectly. There is a simple rule that should eliminate errors with quotes.

The ninth pitfall: Using "like" instead of "as" or "as if" when a preposition is required. Like the split infinitive, this is a relatively minor mistake, but the amount of publicity given it makes it a good one to avoid.

The tenth pitfall: Using words that do not exist, words that do not mean what you think they do, and words that belong only in poetry.

Each of these pitfalls is worth examining in some detail.

SPOTTING YOUR MISTAKES ═══════════════

Unless you recognize these ten common errors when you see them, it will be hard to correct them. Therefore, a sample letter containing at least one fairly common example of each of the ten errors is shown here. The letter is loaded with mistakes. See if you can spot them. Then, as you continue through this chapter, notice boxed corrections at the beginning of each section.

Mr. Z. Wellington Zap
Pawls 'n Mauls. Inc.
24 Barrington Boulevard
Buffalo, New York 19400

Dear Mr. Zap:

In your letter of July 24th you	1
inferred that I seem disinterested	2
in buying gross lots of cast iron	3
pawls from your company. This is	4
not wholly true, and needless to say	5
I would like to verbally discuss the	6
retail pawl market with you sometime	7
in the near future. It is quite	8
important to me.	9
Like my former boss always said	10
ere he kicked the proverbial bucket,	11
"You can't sell what you don't stock".	12
Since I think I can sell your pawls,	13
I will have to stock them, irregard-	14
less of my personal opinion of their	15
merit. Each of us are going to lose	16
money by letting the competition	17
steal a march on us.	18

Sincerely,

A. Stoningham Arp
Vice President
Ratchets Unlimited

HOW TO CHOOSE THE RIGHT WORD ════════

> See the sample letter: Line 2—"inferred" Line 6—"verbally"
>
> - *Inferred* is a commonly misused word, an "almost right" word. The right word is *implied*. The writer of a letter implies something; his reader infers it. You imply (hint or suggest); I infer (draw a conclusion).
> - *Verbally*, strictly speaking, means "by the use of words." It does not mean the same thing as *orally*. Since it is impossible to discuss something any way but verbally, Mr. Arp should have said "orally" or "in person"—or left the word out entirely.

Here are three tips that should help you in choosing the right word:

1. Know the exact meanings of all words you commit to paper.
2. Reread what you have written.
3. Put yourself in the prospective reader's shoes by asking yourself, "Is what I have said absolutely clear?"

There is no excuse for using "almost right" words. You have a large enough vocabulary to say precisely what you mean, and it should never be necessary to take chances with words whose meanings are unclear to you. When in doubt, use a word you know or else check the dictionary.

Choosing the right word also means using the shortest and commonest word in most cases. It means using *after* instead of *subsequent to, end* instead of *finalize, soon* instead of *momentarily, try* instead of *endeavor*, and *stop* instead of *terminate*.

Pompous writing is dull, second-rate writing. If you make it a point to use words that mean something to you, words that are simple and direct, you will not confuse either yourself or your readers. Putting across your message should be your sole aim. "Fine" writing should be left to the novelists. Obscure writing should be left to sociologists and mystics.

LOWERING THE CLICHÉ COUNT

> Sample letter: line 11—"kicked the proverbial bucket" line 18—"steal a march"
>
> - *Kicked the bucket* is trite, and Arp knows it. So what does he do? He puts in *proverbial* and makes his hackneyed phrase sound all the more hackneyed.
> - *Steal a march* is a borderline case. Some readers may find it lively and expressive. Others may feel it is no better than *kick the bucket*. Which proves it is not always easy to tell what is a cliché and what isn't.

Trying to avoid using clichés in your writing is like trying to dodge raindrops in a cloudburst. We all think in clichés, speak in clichés, and write in clichés. That's why there are so many writers and so few poets. To say something supremely and memorably well demands a touch of genius. Most of us don't have it; but, of course, we don't need it.

Still, it is hardly necessary for any normal adult to use as many clichés as an average teenager or a punch-drunk boxer. Many people do, though. With a little thought you can eliminate a good many hackneyed expressions from your writing. Whenever you find yourself overusing certain phrases—and everyone does this—make it a point to get rid of these phrases. You will be surprised at how much better your writing will sound.

OMITTING NEEDLESS WORDS

> Sample letter: line 5—"needless to say" line 6—"verbally" (see page 58)
>
> - *Needless to say* is superfluous. If something is not worth saying, why say it?

The authors of a leading college handbook of English composition give an illustration to show the acceptability of ending a sentence with a preposition. Their rule is all right. But notice the sample sentence the college professor uses to prove their point: "This is a picture of the woman I am in love with." Good grief! Why use the preposition at all? Surely the sentence would have been better as, "This is a picture of the woman I love." Fewer words, stronger sentence.

Wordiness, it seems, is prevalent even among English teachers. Certainly it is a common ailment among the rest of us. Where is the person who has never said "at the present time" instead of "now" or "due to the fact that" instead of "because"? Some wordiness is unavoidable unless you hire a full-time editor. But there are many common, unnecessary expressions which you can avoid with a minimum of effort. Your writing will improve markedly if you eliminate them. Here are a few:

Wordy	Better
in the not too distant future	soon
a sufficient number of	enough
during the period from	from
to the effect that	that
during the course of	during
in the immediate vicinity of	near
in most cases	usually
along the lines of	similar to
in excess of	more than
somewhere in the neighborhood of	about or approximately
in order to	to
refer back to	refer to

Remember, as a general rule: The fewest words equals the best writing.

SINGULAR SUBJECT, SINGULAR VERB FORM

Sample letter: line 16—"each of us are going to lose"

- The words *each* and *either* require the singular verb form "Each of us is going to lose. . ."

Usually, common sense will be a better guide than strict rules when it comes to making a subject and verb agree. However, there are two tricky problems that sometimes arise:

1. Hard-to-Find Subjects

Many people go astray when they try to write a sentence like this: "The word of two teachers, three judges, and four clergymen (is or are) sufficient." It should be *is*, of course, since the subject of the sentence is *word*. But it's very easy to forget about the subject when you have just written three plural nouns before coming to the verb. Rereading is essential in such cases.

2. Collective Nouns

Collective nouns are those that refer to a group of people. Well-known examples are *team*, *jury*, and *class*. The rule for them, while easy to state, is often hard to apply. Here it is: When the group is regarded as a unit, the verb is singular—"The jury was out for one hour." When the members of the group are thought of as individuals, the verb is plural—"The jury were wrangling for hours over the evidence." (Note, however, that it's often more sensible to change *jury* to *jury members*, *team* to *members of the team*, etc.)

If you know the rule and write carefully, you should be able to decide whether a collective noun is being used as a singular or as a plural subject.

THE SPLIT INFINITIVE

Sample letter: line 6—"to verbally discuss"

- *To verbally discuss* is a split infinitive. The infinitive is *to* plus the verb *discuss*; the word *verbally* breaks it in half. An infinitive is easily recognized; it is the "to" form of the verb: *to go, to write, to fly*. Infinitives are easy to split: *to never go, to seldom write*, and *to immediately fly*. But remember: Split infinitives are sometimes better than self-conscious "corrections" of them.

It is often impossible *not* to split an infinitive without also wrecking a sentence. Let's look at an example: *"To legally abolish all rules of grammar is impossible."* How can you change that sentence? How can you kill the split infinitive without abandoning common sense? You would have to write a tortured and foolish sentence. Don't do it.

The one strong argument against separating *to* from the verb is that to do so usually makes an awkward sounding sentence. *To clumsily operate, to speedily process,* or *to superficially study* aren't right *because they don't sound right.* The words are simply in the wrong order.

The best habit for a person interested in grammar to cultivate is to listen with the "mind's ear" when rereading what he or she has written. This will take care of all the bad split infinitives. And who cares to argue about the acceptable ones?

STAMPING OUT THE MYSTERIOUS "IT"

Sample letter: line 8—"It is quite important to me"

- But just *what* is "quite important" to Mr. Arp? The retail pawl market? The discussion with Mr. Zap? No one knows. The word *it* does not clearly refer to anything. In the words of the grammarians, Mr. Arp's "it" has ambiguous reference.

Brevity may be the soul of wit, but brevity plus clarity is the soul of business writing. Whenever you use the word *it* or *that* or *this,* make absolutely certain the pronoun refers to one definite previous word or thought. If there is any ambiguity at all, *repeat the phrase* and *eliminate the pronoun.*

A lot of nonsense has been written about the necessity of varying sentence structure. Presumably you add interest by adding variety, and pronouns are the commonest tools for the job. But if you sacrifice understanding, you gain nothing. Pronouns properly used are a useful kind of shorthand; improperly used they are a reader's nightmare.

The only rule for avoiding ambiguous reference is this: Reread what you have written. (How many times have we said *that?*) Put yourself in the reader's shoes. Make sure you haven't thrown him or her a mysterious *it* or *that* or *this*. Every pronoun must refer to an obvious antecedent.

How could Mr. Arp have corrected his sentence? He could have said, "Such a discussion is quite important to me." Or "The retail pawl market is quite important to me." By eliminating the mysterious *it*—and repeating the intended antecedent—he would have made his meaning clear.

A SIMPLE RULE FOR APOSTROPHES ═══════════

Sample letter: inside address—"Pawls 'n Mauls"

- In contractions, an apostrophe takes the place of a missing letter or a continuous group of letters. "Pawls 'n' Mauls" (with two apostrophes) would therefore be correct. This is a missing *a*, a written *n* and then a missing *d*. Both missing letters must be replaced by apostrophes.

Contractions are easy. Possessive nouns, however, do not seem quite so easy, and many people balk when it comes to making possessives out of such words as *Thomas, waitress,* or *people.* Should it be *Thomas' job,* or *Thomas's job,* or *Thomases' job.* . .or what?

Actually, the rule for possessives is fairly simple, if the once-in-a-million exceptions are ignored. Once you learn the basic rule, you should never make a serious mistake with apostrophes Here is the rule:

Singular possessives: Write the singular form of the noun (e.g. John, person, Dickens), then add *'s* (e.g., John's, person's, Dickens's).
Plural possessives: Write the plural form of the noun (e.g., women, Joneses), then. .
  a. If the plural form of the noun does not end in *s,* add *'s* just as in the singular (e.g. women's)
  b. If the plural form of the noun does end in *s,* add only an apostrophe (e.g., Joneses')

Note: Before you even think about the apostrophe, write the form of the noun, singular or plural, that you wish to use. Then you simply add 's, with this one exception: If the noun is *plural* and *already ends in* "s", just tack on an apostrophe.

Long lists of complicated rules have been written on how to put apostrophes in possessives, but the one given here can almost never lead you astray. Watch:

Singular form of noun	Singular possessive	Plural form of noun	Plural possessive
Thomas	Thomas's	Thomases	Thomases'
boy	boy's	boys	boys'
waitress	waitress's	waitresses	waitresses'
person	person's	people	people's
child	child's	children	children's

"WHERE DO I PUT THE QUOTATION MARKS?"

Sample letter: line 12—"what you don't stock".

- Quotation marks always go outside the period. AL-WAYS. (For example: Mr. Smith wrote the letter "e.")The length of a quote has no bearing whatever on this rule.

There is little excuse for making mistakes with quotation marks, for the rules governing them could hardly be easier. Here they are:

1. *Period.* Quotation marks *always* go *outside* the period (e.g., His lawyer called the charge "a phantasm.")
2. *Comma.* Quotation marks *always* go *outside* the comma, just as with the period. (e.g., The vice-president's yachts are named "Moe," "Flo," and "Zoe.")
3. *Semicolon.* Quotation marks *never* go outside the semicolon. (e.g., The statement referred to Mr. Burns as "an absolute idiot"; otherwise it was inaccurate.)

4. *Question Mark.* This is the only one that's a bit tricky:
   a. If the whole, verbatim question is quoted, quotation marks go *outside* the question mark. (e.g., My friend asked, "What is that mushroom cloud on the horizon?")
   b. If the whole, verbatim question is *not* quoted, quotation marks go inside the question mark. (e.g., Didn't Bill say something about "a mushroom cloud on the horizon"?)

The rules given above are simplified, and an English teacher might take exception to them because of that one unusual time when they may be wrong. However, as a working guide, they are well-nigh perfect.

LIKE AND AS

Sample letter: line 10—"Like my former boss always said"

• *Like* should be *as.* "As my former boss always said. . ."

The solution to the "like" or "as" problem lies not so much in knowing what a preposition is, or what a conjunction is, as in knowing what a *verb* is. Generally speaking, the verb holds the key to *like* or *as.*

• If a verb follows the word in question (*like* or *as*), you will usually need *as.*
• If a verb does *not* follow the word in question (*like* or *as*), you will usually need *like.*

As

As I *was telling* you, he's a good salesman.
      verb
It is the only solution, *as* I've always maintained.
                                verb

Like

He went quite slowly, *like* the rest of them.

If you were to add the verb *did* at the end of this sentence, you would have to change the *like* to *as*—a good illustration of the verb rule in action.

SOME WORDS THAT BEAR WATCHING ═══════

Sample letter: line 14—"irregardless" line 2—"disinterested" line 11—"ere"

- *Irregardless* is a nonexistent word among educated people. The proper word is *regardless*.
- *Disinterested* means unbiased or unselfish—nothing else. The correct word for *not interested* is *uninterested*.
- *Ere* is all right for poetry but stilted for most other kinds of writing.

Nearly every book of English grammar contains a glossary of frequently misused words. There is not enough space in this book to list more than a very few, but, surprisingly enough, only a few seem to crop up again and again. Here are some of them:

Alright. There is no such word. It must be written *all right*.

And etc. *And* with *etc.* is superfluous. It should be just *etc*.

Enthuse. Not a good word. It should be replaced with "becomes enthusiastic" or with a substitute verb.

It's. This is a contraction and means nothing except "it is." Don't use *it's* in place of *its*, the possessive pronoun.

Less. The word *less* concerns "value," "degree," or "amount." *Fewer* should be used with numbers.

Muchly. Not a good word. Use *much*.

TEN TIPS FOR MASTERING EVERYDAY ENGLISH

1. Don't guess at word meanings when you write. Use only words you can define.

2. Get rid of expressions you tend to overuse. Develop alternate words and phrases for them.

3. Reread everything you write and delete extraneous words.

4. Make certain the subject and verb agree in each sentence you write.

5. Learn to recognize split infinitives and avoid using them when they sound awkward.

6. Make sure every *it, that,* or *this* refers unmistakably to a noun farther back in the sentence.

7. Learn the rule for apostrophes in possessive nouns. Add *'s* unless you have a plural noun already ending in *s;* then add just an apostrophe.

8. Always put quotation marks *outside* the comma and the period.

9. Don't use *like* interchangeably with *as.* Look for the verb.

10. Eliminate such abominations as *irregardless, alright,* and *muchly.*

Chapter 6

Shortcuts in Mental Arithmetic

69

BILL CERNAK, A YOUNG SUPERINTENDENT in a glass bottle factory, tells how he amazed a new employee with a simple calculation in math.

"It's hard to believe," he says, "but Ted, a high school graduate, could barely add 10 and 10 in his head. When it came to figuring his daily output of beer cartons, Ted, who worked in the carton department, was completely lost. The cartons are shipped flat and then stapled together by us; they come bundled in groups of 25. At the end of his first day I asked Ted how many cartons he had done. He looked at me in bewilderment.

" 'I don't know,' he said. 'I've done 17 bundles.'

" 'Well,' I said, 'that's 425. Not bad. The quota's 550, and you can probably make that by the end of the week.'

"He looked at me suspiciously. 'Do you have all those numbers memorized?' he asked.

" 'No,' I said, 'but it's easy to multiply *any* number by 25.'

" 'Come off it,' he said. 'What's 25 times 38?'

" '950,' I answered immediately. Ted took a pencil from his pocket and wrote on a nearby carton:

$$
\begin{array}{r}
25 \\
\times\ \ 38 \\
\hline
200 \\
75 \\
\hline
950
\end{array}
$$

"He looked at me in astonishment, then said, 'My God, you're right.' And from that day to this he has called me 'The Whiz.' I only wish he had given me a few harder problems: 25 times 760 or 25 times 136. Then he really would have been impressed!"

Probably so. But mental arithmetic of this kind is just as easy as Bill Cernak finds it. That's not true of the phenomenal kinds of arithmetical calculations, of course—2762 times 1983 times 6114, and that sort of thing. Only a real genius can work those mentally. But it is true of the average day-to-day calculations that everyone has to make.

A few basic rules can enable you to solve most simple math problems in your head. And, happily, you don't have to be a mathematical marvel.

SIMPLIFY, SIMPLIFY, SIMPLIFY

The cardinal rule of mental arithmetic is this: Simplify anything that can possibly be simplified. At first this may sound like rather mysterious advice, but as you go along in the chapter, you will see what I mean.

Let's start with addition.

There is nothing difficult about addition. Anyone can do it, and most people can do it quite quickly—on paper. However, I suspect there are few people who can keep up *mentally* with the cash register at a supermarket. Yet it's actually possible to do this, within reasonable limits, once you learn how to simplify the major problem in addition.

The major problem can be stated in one word: carrying. If every problem were as easy as the following one, you would never find yourself in trouble:

$$
\begin{array}{r}
71 \\
+\quad 20 \\
\hline
\end{array}
$$

To add these numbers, all you have to do is add 7 and 2, then add 1 and 0, to get the answer: 91. Notice that I proceeded from *left to right*. This is an important point to keep in mind, for when you learned addition in school, you always worked in the opposite direction, from right to left. Why change now? Simply because all answers in addition *read* from the left, and the answer to the problem above was not 1 and then 9; it was 9 and then 1, or 91. Therefore, if you can always read numbers from the left when adding—and you can—the digits will be in "normal" order.

Even a problem that looks hard may yield a quick and easy answer:

$$64381$$
$$+\ 23604$$

You will see at a glance that none of the columns in this problem will add to more than 9. Consequently, you can instantly reel off the answer. You don't have to add the digits in reverse. Merely add 6 and 2, then 4 and 3, then 3 and 6, and so on. Presto! The answer is 87985.

There is a drawback, of course. Very often one of the columns will add to more than 9. What then? What then indeed. This is precisely the reason you were taught to add in school by working in reverse. Working in reverse, from right to left, will allow you to carry.

HOW TO AVOID CARRYING

There is a way to avoid carrying in addition, and it is well worth learning. Suppose you are faced with the following problem:

$$58$$
$$+\ 26$$

The 8 and 6 will add to 14. Then you will have to carry that pesky 1 into the left-hand column—and possibly get confused in the process. Don't do it. Simplify. *Don't add 58 and 26 at all.* Add two numbers that are easier to add. No, I'm not kidding. Take the number that ends with the highest last digit (in this case 58) and mentally change it to the next highest number ending in 0 (in this case 60). It would be a cinch to add 60 and 26, wouldn't it? Certainly, you say, but those are not the numbers I'm adding. Right. But you know that you've added 2 to your 58. Just as easily you can *take away* 2 from your 26. Therefore, you are adding not 58 and 26 but *60 and 24*. Even Ted, the carton man, could do that mentally: 84.

With this technique, you have eliminated the problem of

carrying. You have simplified. Now try the technique on the following problem:

$$\begin{array}{ccc} 49 & 77 & 48 \\ +\ 22 & +16 & +34 \\ \hline \end{array}$$

Easy, wasn't it? Still, if you are reasonably good in math, this procedure may seem pointless. You may already be able to carry numbers in your head. However, the basic technique will also work with problems in which you can't carry the numbers in your head. For instance:

$$\begin{array}{c} 798 \\ +\ 113 \\ \hline \end{array}$$

By adding 2 to the entire top number (making it 800) and by deducting 2 from 113 (making it 111), you can rattle off the answer, 911, without a moment's hesitation.

Try the same technique with the following problems:

$$\begin{array}{ccc} 697 & 396 & 599 \\ +\ 283 & +\ 208 & +\ 417 \\ \hline \end{array}$$

It really does work, but there is one word of caution. The method does not work very often with large numbers; not even, in fact, the three-digit numbers. However, most of the numbers you add in everyday life are not large numbers. And a person who masters this method can easily add five or six or even more grocery prices in his or her head. Watch:

$$\begin{array}{ll}
58\} & \\
34\} & 58 \text{ plus } 34 \text{ becomes } 60 \text{ plus } 32 = 92 \\
19\} & 92 \text{ plus } 19 \text{ becomes } 91 \text{ plus } 20 = 111 \\
26\} & 111 \text{ plus } 26 \text{ (no carrying)} = 137 \\
35\} & 137 \text{ plus } 35 \text{ becomes } 140 \text{ plus } 32 = 172 \\
98\} & 172 \text{ plus } 98 \text{ becomes } 170 \text{ plus } 100 = 270 \\
\end{array}$$

HOW ABOUT AN ESTIMATE? ═══════════════

We have been talking about *exact* answers to problems in addition. But exact answers aren't always necessary. Suppose, for example, an office manager wants to acquire seven personal computer systems. The systems she is offered vary in capability and price, but the manager knows she doesn't want to pay more than $30,000 for all of them. The salesperson has listed the prices this way:

> System 1— $4,200
> System 2—　3,650
> System 3—　6,175
> System 4—　4,200
> System 5—　5,875
> System 6—　6,900
> System 7—　3,500

It is not necessary for the manager to add these figures exactly. All she has to do is run quickly through the thousands column: 4, 3, 6, 4, 5, 6, and 3. The total is 31, or *at least $31,000.* Instantly the manager decides that she is not willing to pay the asking prices for the computer systems.

Even had the total come to 30 exactly, the manager would know that any prices containing hundreds would put the asking price for the computers over $30,000.

You will encounter many situations that do not require an exact total. When you do, however, it is sensible to follow the builder's lead. Simplify the problem. After doing so, you may discover that you do need an exact total. If so, you can take the steps required to get it. But there is no reason to spend time adding complex figures that do not need to be added.

My wife uses a method of mental estimation when she is shopping. If our semi weekly budget allows $120 for groceries, for instance, she rounds off each individual price to *ten.* Then she keeps a running total as she is putting items into the cart. This way she can easily come quite close to the final total. Here is an illustration of her method:

Actual price	Adjusted price	Running total
$.49	$.50	$ .50
.61	.60	1.10
2.68	2.70	3.80
.37	.40	4.20
.65	.70	4.90
1.09	1.10	6.00
4.89	4.90	10.90
.64	.60	11.50
.53	.50	12.00

Since the actual price of all the items is $11.95, she has come within five cents of being right on the nose. And that's close enough for her purposes.

Remember: Unless you need an exact total—and there are many cases where you don't—use a simple method of estimating. It may be necessary to add only the thousands column or the hundreds column to get a rough estimate; or, it may be necessary to round off figures in your head and thus keep a simple running total.

A SHORTCUT IN SUBTRACTION

While in addition the main problem is carrying, in subtraction it is borrowing. As long as borrowing is not involved, you can work a subtraction problem (again from left to right) with lightning speed:

$$\begin{array}{r} 839 \\ -\ 514 \\ \hline \end{array}$$

5 from 8 is 3, 1 from 3 is 2, and 4 from 9 is 5; and the instantaneous answer is 325. But as soon as you have to borrow, the problem becomes more complicated, and you can no longer merely read off the answer. There is, however, an easy method for subtracting two- and three-digit numbers in your head. This method simplifies this problem by making borrowing unnecessary. Watch:

$$\begin{array}{r} 76 \\ -\ 28 \\ \hline \end{array}$$

In school you would have said, "8 from 16 is 8; then 2 from 7 minus 1, or 2 from 6, is 4." The answer arrived at by working backwards—that is, from right to left—is 48.

In the simplified method, you *add* something to the bottom number so as to make it end in 0. In this case you add 2, giving you 30 instead of 28. Now, 30 would be easy to take away from 76, wouldn't it? "Of course," you say, "but doing so would give me the wrong answer." Yes indeed. You must therefore adjust the other figure. In order to keep the basic problem the same, you must *add the same number to both figures in the problem.* Thus:

$$
\begin{array}{c}
76 \\[-2pt]
\text{becomes} \\[-2pt]
-\ 28
\end{array}
\qquad
\begin{array}{c}
(+2) \quad 78 \\[6pt]
(+2)\ -\ 30
\end{array}
$$

Instantly you can see that the answer is 48. No borrowing is involved, and the last column is always easy to work with since it contains a 0 to be taken from the top number. Try this technique on these problems:

$$
\begin{array}{ccc}
73 & 84 & 47 \\
-\ 27 & -\ 39 & -\ 18
\end{array}
$$

Notice, incidentally, that you *always* add to the *bottom* number, even though the last digit of it may be small:

$$
\begin{array}{c}
51 \\[-2pt]
\text{becomes} \\[-2pt]
-\ 23
\end{array}
\qquad
\begin{array}{c}
(+7) \quad 58 \\[6pt]
(+7)\ -\ 30
\end{array}
$$

When this method is used with three-digit numbers, a second step is sometimes desirable:

$$
\begin{array}{c}
611 \\[-2pt]
\text{becomes} \\[-2pt]
-\ 488
\end{array}
\quad
\begin{array}{c}
(+2) \quad 613 \\[-2pt]
\text{becomes} \\[-2pt]
(+2)\ -490
\end{array}
\quad
\begin{array}{c}
(+10) \quad 623 \\[6pt]
(+10)\ -\ 500
\end{array}
$$

At first this may seem like a complicated way to solve fairly simple problems in subtraction. However, if you practice the method, you will find that it is really quite easy. You will also find that it permits you to solve, quickly and in your head, most of the day-to-day problems in subtraction.

Here are a few more subtraction problems for practice and review:

56	84	91
− 29	− 36	− 68

72	63	45
− 43	− 25	− 17

855	392	644
− 479	− 197	− 278

MULTIPLICATION: THE RULE OF ZEROS

"Many people seem to think," says Mary McGraw, an electrical engineer, "that the multiplication table represents the be-all and end-all of mental math. All of the workers in my factory can multiply 8 times 3. Yet just the other day we had a problem involving nothing more than 8 times 3, and I was the only person around who could solve it mentally.

"We had 800 cartons of transistors. Each carton contained 300 transistors. One of my workers scratched his head and said he thought we had 24,000 transistors. Another had no idea how many there were. Still another sat down and went through the following incredible process on paper:

$$
\begin{array}{r}
800 \\
\times\,300 \\
\hline
000 \\
000 \\
2400 \\
\hline
240000
\end{array}
$$

His answer of 240,000 was right, sure enough, but I was astonished that he had never been told how to *count zeros*. A glance at the answer of 240,000, I said, would show him that the answer has the same number of zeros as the problem itself:

$$
\begin{array}{ccc}
\overset{12}{800} & \overset{34}{\times\ 300} & \overset{1\,234}{=\ 240,000}
\end{array}
$$

"He admitted that it did, but could not believe that merely counting the zeros in both figures of the problem would give him the number of zeros in the answer. It does, though, as I finally convinced him. *Always*. And even if the answer of the multiplication involved has a zero in it—800 × 500, for example—I pointed out that this does not affect the proper number of zeros *to be added*: 5 × 8 = 40. Add four zeros. 40 + *0000*, or 400,000.

"I told him, too, that the size of the problem has no bearing on its difficulty. It's as easy to multiply 800,000 times 30,000 as it is to multiply 800 times 300. All you have to do is count the zeros, and if you know the following table, you can give the answer without batting an eyelash:

```
5,    0  0  0,    0  0  0,    0  0  0
│     │  │  │     │  │  │     │  │  │
b     h  t  m     h  t  t     h  t  u
i     u  e  i     u  e  h     u  e  n
l     n  n  l     n  n  o     n  s  i
l     d     l     d     u     d        t
i     r  m  i     r  t  s     r        s
o     e  i  o     e  h  a     e
n     d  l  n     d  o  n     d
s     m  l  s     t  u  d     s
      i  i        h  s  s
      l  o        o  a
      l  n        u  n
      i  s        s  d
      o           a  s
      n           n
      s           d
                  s
```

5,	0	0	0,	0	0	0,	0	0	0
billions	hundred millions	ten millions	millions	hundred thousands	ten thousands	thousands	hundreds	tens	units

12 345   6 789
"In short, the answer to 800,000 times 30,000 is 24 billion
123 456 789
(24,000,000,000). Very impressive. And very simple."

Try your hand at the following problems:

$$
\begin{array}{ccc}
600 & 5000 & 40000 \\
\times\ 200 & \times\ 300 & \times\ 7000
\end{array}
$$

SIMPLIFIED MULTIPLICATION

Even people with high intelligence often have trouble with problems like 11 times 24. It is difficult to see why. Anyone can multiply 10 times 24. But when the units column has a number other than 0, people seem to become confused. They do not see that they could simplify the problem with no effort at all. With this particular problem it's merely a matter of saying, "10 times 24 is 240, then 1 times 24 is 24, and 240 plus 24 is 264; so that's the answer."

Take another example: 12 times 37. Well, 10 times 37 is 370, then 2 times 37 is 74, and 370 plus 74 is 444. You will have to admit that this is a lot easier than attempting the usual process in your head:

$$
\begin{array}{r}
37 \\
\times\,12 \\
\hline
74 \\
37 \\
\hline
444
\end{array}
$$

You will notice, however, that we've dealt only with 11 and 12—numbers ending in 1 and 2. Wouldn't you run into trouble if you tried to multiply numbers with larger last digits? Not necessarily. Take 19 times 28. In this problem, both of the final digits are large. All right, why not multiply *20* times 28 and then *subtract* that extra 28? Thus, 20 times 28 is 560. But in order to simplify the problem you have used an extra 28. You must now *take away* that 28 from the total: 560 minus 28 (or 562 minus 30— see pages 76–77) gives you 532.

The main thing to remember is this: Simplify the problem. Break a hard multiplication problem into two easy ones. It will take some common sense to do this properly. But once you master the method, you will find its applications obvious.

Test yourself on these problems:

$$
\begin{array}{cccc}
32 & 81 & 16 & 23 \\
\times\,11 & \times\,12 & \times\,22 & \times\,18
\end{array}
$$

THE RULE OF 25

There is one more technique in multiplication that is worth mentioning. It's the one Bill Cernak used to multiply 25 times 17. Whenever you are faced with the number 25, you should remember that 25 is one fourth of 100. Since 25 is ¼ of 100, if you *divide* the other number in the problem by 4, you can reach a quick answer. Bill Cernak thought to himself, "4 into 17 is 4 and ¼. Translated, this is 400 plus ¼ of 100, or 25. The answer, then, is 425."

This method can be used with much more difficult problems, too, if you can divide mentally by 4. Thus, 25 times 760 becomes 4 into 760, or 190. Translated back into hundreds—by adding two zeros—the answer is 19,000. Or take 25 times 324. The problem becomes 4 into 324, or 81. Add two zeros and you have 8,100.

Sometimes you will find this "rule of 25" more trouble than it's worth, particularly if the other number is not exactly divisible by 4. However, the technique is often useful. Try the rule of 2^5 on these problems:

$$\begin{array}{ccc} 64 & 14 & 260 \\ \times\ 25 & \times\ 25 & \times\ 25 \end{array}$$

YES, BUT . . .

It would be misleading to say that mental arithmetic of this kind is as easy as shelling peas. First of all, the methods do take real awareness of how numbers can be manipulated. That is to say, you must have at least a rudimentary understanding of mathematics. You must also be able to "see" the way to handle a particular problem. If you try the wrong approach on it, you will get the wrong answer—or perhaps no answer at all. Also, sometimes more than one mental step is required in the process. If so, you must be able to hold two- and three-digit numbers in your memory.

Above all, you will probably have to practice working mentally with numbers. While addition and subtraction are comparatively easy, multiplication is not. And division is so complex that it would be impossible to cover it in this book.

A final reminder: Unless you are willing to devise your own problems and then try to solve them, you will be likely to run into trouble with actual at-home or on-the-job questions. The techniques of mental arithmetic are helpful, but they are not magic. They take thought and effort.

EIGHT TIPS FOR MENTAL ARITHMETIC

1. Simplify every math problem that can possibly be simplified.

2. In mental addition, if carrying is necessary, change the figure ending in the highest digit to the next highest number ending in 0. Then subtract the same amount from the other figure, and add.

3. Make a quick, reasonable estimate whenever an exact total is not needed.

4. In mental subtraction, if borrowing is necessary, change the bottom figure to the next highest number ending in 0. Then add the same amount to the top figure and subtract.

5. In mental multiplication, if both numbers end in zeros, count the zeros and add them to the answer obtained by simple multiplication.

6. Whenever possible, break a difficult multiplication problem into two easier ones. Then add (or, if required, subtract) the two answers.

7. Learn the "rule of 25" in mental multiplication. Remember that 25 is one fourth of 100, and that an answer can be obtained by dividing by 4, then adding two zeros (or fractional 25s) to this result.

8. In order to master mental arithmetic, keep working at it every day. Make up problems of your own to solve.

Part 2

The Dynamics of Memory

The memory strengthens as
you lay burdens on it, and
becomes trustworthy
as you trust it.

—THOMAS DE QUINCEY

Chapter 7

How to Learn and Remember Names

- Hear the Name
- Repetition Is Vital
- Associating the Name
- Use Mental Pictures
- The Time and Place for Mental Pictures
- Write It Down
- People Are the Keynote
- Learn a Name a Day
- Ten Tips for Learning and Remembering Names

"**I** CAN'T SEEM TO REMEMBER YOUR NAME" is about the costliest sentence there is. It can cost a salesperson an order. It can cost a business executive the loyalty of a subordinate. It can cost a teacher the respect of a student. And it's safe to say that if you use this sentence, ever, it will cost you a friend.

Why is it, then, that so many people go blithely along, forgetting names, forgetting faces, losing orders, losing loyalty and respect, losing friends, and sometimes even losing jobs? The answer is easy enough: Remembering names and faces is work; it requires application and effort; above all, it requires knowledge of how *not* to forget.

Just as you have learned how to do mental arithmetic, you can learn how to remember names and faces. Let's begin. . .

HEAR THE NAME

Mel Forsythe is an easygoing insurance salesperson. He almost seems to pride himself on the fact that he can't remember names from one day to the next. He tries to pass this failing off as a joke. It doesn't work. As a consequence, Mel can't pride himself on the section of town he lives in, on his yearly income, or on his chances for promotion. What Mel Forsythe doesn't seem to realize is that there is a close connection between his failure to remember names and his failure to make big money.

There's another salesperson in Mel's company who knows what it means to remember names. She's Janet Finnegan, and her income is about three times as high as Mel's. Janet's future is bright. What's her memory secret?

"It's no secret," says Janet. "There's one sure way to remember names. It works for me and it pays me cash dividends. I listen to a person's name when I'm introduced to him or her. I figure if I don't hear the name in the first place, I'll never to able to remember it later. So I listen. I listen hard."

Janet is right. "Listening hard" is the first step in remembering names and faces, and it's important. If you don't ever hear the name in the first place, you will not remember it. Does this seem obvious? Probably. But how many times have you seen two people being introduced. . .One person is staring past the other at a picture on the wall, the other is nodding absently and fiddling with a ring. Such an introduction is a waste of time. Obviously neither of these people will remember the other's name, and then they will wonder why!

"I can't remember names," says Mel Forsythe. Very likely he doesn't even listen to names. He doesn't catch them in the first place.

This rule should be etched in your mind. Listen to names. *Listen* to them Ask that the name be repeated if you miss it the first time. Ask the person to spell the name if it is a difficult one. Don't worry about offending the host or the person to whom you are introduced. Both will be flattered. Both will know that you're making an honest effort to learn the name.

By all means heed Oliver Wendell Holmes's words: "A man must *get* a thing before he can *forget* it."

REPETITION IS VITAL

In learning new vocabulary words, you will find that repeating them is vital. The same holds true in learning and remembering someone's name.

Watch someone who's good at names in action. As soon as she's introduced, she'll acknowledge it with a "Very pleased to meet you, Mr. Barton," or with a similar comment. She'll say the person's name *immediately*. Then Mr. Barton's name will pop into the conversation at virtually every succeeding sentence. When they part, the last remark will be something like, "I hope we meet again, Mr. Barton." The good name-person will have used Mr. Barton's name as many times as possible. Repetition, as we said before, is the key to retention.

Some people say they are uneasy about using a person's name so many times at the first meeting. Nothing could be sillier. It's an adage as old as humankind that everyone loves the sound of his own name. He loves it whether he hears it from a genius or a fool, from a friend or an enemy, from a stranger of a lover. Overusing names is impossible. Try to remember the last time you were offended by a person using your name too often. I'll bet you can't.

ASSOCIATING THE NAME

If you ever meet a man who is about six feet four inches tall, with a short dark beard, sunken cheeks, and careworn eyes, and his name turns out to be Arthur Lincoln, I'm sure you'll remember his name—or at least his last name.

This is a rather far-fetched example of what is meant by "associating" the name. Unhappily, it will rarely be quite that easy. George Black may have blue eyes, blond hair, a red tie, a gray suit, and brown shoes.

But there is no question about the usefulness of this technique. For one thing, it forces you to think about the person to whom you are being introduced. It forces you to look closely at her, to think about her name and about her. It carries you one long step beyond the handshaking stage. If there is anything about the sound of the name that seems to fit the appearance or personality of the person, you will easily make usable associations. Mr. Earhardt may have prominent, or at least distinctive, ears. Mrs. Pierce may have a shrill, piercing voice.

An association may be amusing, even outlandish. Psychologists tell us that we remember humorous and improbable mental pictures more easily than "sensible" ones. So let your imagination loose; make associations between names and appearances—and make them as wild as you wish.

Now, some names are easier to associate than others. Names that involve colors—Mr. Gray, Mrs. Green, Ms. Redmond—are easy to associate with physical appearances. (Incidentally, concerning Mr. Black, who was mentioned earlier, the fact that nothing about him *was* black is an association in itself.) Names that involve occupations—Mr. Carpenter, Mrs. Goldsmith, Ms. Farmer—are quite easy. Names that involve mental or personality traits—Mr. Manley, Ms. Huff, Ms. Pride—are usually easy.

Names that clearly indicate national orgins—Mr. Rizzo, Ms. O'Grady, Miss Mueller—can be used if the person has characteristics normally associated with people from that country. Of course, the association will not be quite as close as with colors, occupations, or traits. Nationality is merely a clue to the name, not the name itself.

It should be mentioned that *parts* of names are often sufficient for purposes of association. With Mr. Pepitone, the "pep' will help. With Mrs. Rosenberg, the "rose" may be enough (but you'll have to remember that Rose is not the whole name). With Ms. Nicolson, the "nickel" may give you some assistance if you can make an association between the coin and the person.

There are limits to this method. Some names—like Mr. Lundquist, Mrs. Lewis, Miss Tyrrell—cannot easily be associated. But you will be amazed at how many *can* be when you make a conscientious effort. And you'll be glad you tried!

USE MENTAL PICTURES

The use of striking mental pictures is so valuable that it is worth examining in more detail.

I once witnessed a memory demonstration by a man named Dwight Ashley. Mr. Ashley was introduced just once to each person in a room containing perhaps 35 people. He took his time with these introductions; he repeated each name once and sometimes twice; occasionally he asked for the spelling. As soon as the introductions were completed, Mr. Ashley had each person stand up—and they stood up in random order—whereupon he repeated the person's name. He did not miss a single one.

How did he do it? Mr. Ashley described his method to the group: "I made an amusing mental picture of each person, a picture that helped me to associate the name with the man. For instance, I remembered Mr. Starrett by putting an angel's *star* over his head. When Mr. Starret stood up, that angel's star rose over him like the eve of the first Christmas. It practically illuminated the room. I couldn't miss it."

Mr. Ashley, an elderly gentleman with a high forehead, suggested that we remember *his* name by picturing a round ash spot, like the ones you see at Eastertime, in the middle of his forehead. He went on to say: "You may think that you still won't remember my name. You'll grope around, you think, and toy with names like Ashton, Ashbury, Ashmoleon. Let me tell you that you won't. All you really need is the first syllable. You'll remember the -*ley* without even trying. After all, a person who forgets a name usually forgets it completely. If he had one syllable to go on, the name would instantly leap to his mind."

I, for one, have never forgotten Mr. Ashley, and I doubt that the others in the room that night have forgotten him either.

It's worth noting, too, that by remembering a person's name, you will very probably remember his or her face. The mere fact that you have once "seen" Mr. Starrett with a glowing star over his head, or Mr. Ashley with the sign of Ash Wednesday on him, will give you a mental picture of the face itself. Therefore, when you see either one again, you are more likely to recognize both the face and the name than you would have been had you not used mental pictures.

THE TIME AND PLACE FOR MENTAL PICTURES

Mental pictures, like all memory devices, are useful under many circumstances. But they are not always necessary. A salesperson or a dentist or a teacher can use them with great profit, for in all of these professions it is essential to remember a great many people who are seen only at intervals.

But it would obviously be foolish for a salesclerk in a hardware store to use them for remembering customers' names. There are just too many small-purchase customers for the process to be practical. On the other hand, it would be extremely worthwhile for a salesclerk in a men's clothing store to use mental pictures for remember the names of her regular customers. It is even safe to bet that if she were to do so, the list of her regular customers would rapidly increase. A person loves to hear his own name spoken, especially by a virtual stranger.

Let's take another illustration. It would be silly to use mental pictures to remember the names of your own children, even if you had fourteen of them. Unless you were a remarkably forgetful parent, you would hardly need mental pictures to key you in on your own offspring. However, I know a parent who uses mental pictures to remember the names of all the *other* children in her neighborhood. As you might guess, she is an exceptionally popular woman—and not just with the children, but also with their proud mothers and dads.

One final word. In using any memory system there is a great temptation to apply artificial mnemonic devices when they are not really needed. Thus, a warning is in order. Determine the people—or, more accurately, the kinds of people—whose names you need to remember. Then use the system of mental pictures solely for them. You will be surprised at how effectively it will work if you limit the number names, take the task seriously, and make up mental pictures that are both amusing and apt.

WRITE IT DOWN

If you have listened carefully to a person's name, repeated is several times, and tried to associate it with his appearance or personality, you should remember it. Probably you will remember the name if you meet the same person tomorrow or the next day. You may remember it even if you meet him a month from now. But time can be the enemy of memory. One way to combat the enemy is by writing down the name at frequent intervals. As you write the name, try to form a mental picture of the person himself. By doing this, you will be able to remember important names even though you do not see the person very frequently.

Another good reason for writing down the name is that it will give you repeated practice in spelling it. As you know, there is nothing more annoying than to receive a letter with your name misspelled on the envelope. Everyone feels the same way about misspelled names. Nor is it pleasant, after your first meeting, to have to ask a person how to spell his name. Most people will think you should know how, and they will be right.

PEOPLE ARE THE KEYNOTE

So far we have talked about remembering names. Now we must talk about remembering people. After all, a name is merely a label; the person behind the label is what counts. Unless you are interested, genuinely interested, in the people you meet, you cannot and will not remember their names.

Being interested in a person means more than just being interested in her name. It means being interested in her appearance, personality, occupation, hobbies, unusual experiences, travels, and much more. It means identifying her as a unique individual. It means liking a person and wanting to learn more about her. If you make an honest effort to learn all you can about each person you meet, you will have little difficulty in remembering names.

The next time you want to remember a person's name, try to learn as much as you can about that person. Ask other people about her. Find out what she likes and dislikes. Try to describe her physical appearance in detail. Not only will this aid you in associating her name with her appearance or personality, it will also make her a more "real" person to you. In short, she will become more than just a name.

LEARN A NAME A DAY

The best way to accomplish any task is to establish a timetable and then stick to it. If you want to increase your ability to learn and remember names, the ideal way is to practice it constantly. And the easiest way to practice is by doing.

Make it a point to try to learn at least one new name every day of the year. This may sound like an impossible job, but it's not. Most people meet at least one new person a day whether they try or not. Certainly if you make a real effort to meet a new person, you will have no trouble doing so.

Of course, there is more than one advantage in learning a new name each day. Probably the least important of these is that you will become more adept at remembering names. Much more important is that your range of acquaintances—people whom you know by name—will become immeasurably broader. Your horizons will expand. You will meet people you have always wanted to know, people whose friendships can be worth a great deal to you.

When you meet each person, follow the steps already outlined: (1) hear the person's name, (2) repeat the name, (3) try to associate the name with a physical or personality trait of the person, (4) write the name down at frequent intervals, (5) find out as much as you can about each person whose name you want to remember.

If you follow this procedure with everyone you meet, you will be amazed at how many people you will get to know—and, just as important, how many people will get to know you.

TEN TIPS FOR LEARNING AND
REMEMBERING NAMES ═══════════════════

1. Decide now to begin learning and remembering the name of each person you meet.

2. Listen carefully to a person's name when you are introduced to her.

3. Ask the person to repeat her name if you fail to get it the first time. Ask her to spell it if it is an unusual name.

4. Repeat the person's name immediately, at the same time you acknowledge the introduction.

5. Keep repeating the name throughout your conversation. Use the name once again at the very end of the conversation.

6. Try to associate the name of every person you meet with some outstanding physical or personality trait.

7. Become acquainted with the distinctive names of people of different national origins.

8. Write down the names of people you meet. Make sure you know how to spell these names.

9. Be genuinely interested in people—their looks, personalities, jobs, and so on.

10. Try to learn at least one new name a day by meeting as many people as possible.

Chapter 8

Remembering Numbers with the Peg Method

A PERSON WITH AN OUTSTANDING MEMORY is usually respected and admired. No doubt this is because a superior memory is so unusual. It attracts attention, even awe, among the great majority of us who find "thirty days hath September" hard to keep straight. Yes, a remarkable memory is a social asset; it accounts, I suspect, for the sales success of many memory courses. The people who buy these courses want very much to appear brilliant, to have their friends and acquaintances "ooh" and "ah" over their apparent genius.

In short, there is a good deal of childishness in the common attitude toward mnemonics, or memory training. The majority of humankind will gaze in wonderment at the person who has memorized the Manhattan telephone directory. Few of them will ask the obvious and sensible question: "Why would anyone want to memorize the Manhattan telephone directory?" Nearly everyone, under these circumstances, overlooks the real purpose of a good memory, which is simply to remember what needs to be remembered.

This chapter sets forth a simple memory system for remembering numbers. It is a system hundreds of years old, and it still works. To illustrate: In college I knew a student who used the system to memorize the exact population of every state in the Union. His classmates considered him a mental wizard. They would shout "Indiana." He would concentrate for a moment, then reply "3,934,224." By now the 1990 census, and common sense as well, have overtaken him. He still uses a memory system, but only sparingly and for numbers that he has a genuine need to remember.

The point is that the "peg method," explained in the following pages, is a useful device for remembering long and difficult numbers. It is an "artificial" method, to be sure, and it will hardly turn you into a wizard overnight. But it is worth knowing and trying.

MAKE USE OF "NATURAL" ASSOCIATIONS

We should begin by saying that it's silly to use an artificial system for memorizing numbers that you can remember anyway. You don't need the peg method to remember your own birthday or the birthdays in your immediate family. Nor do you need it to remember your house number, your bowling average, or your state's speed limit.

There are other numbers that can be remembered easily. These are numbers with "natural" associations. If a relative's house number is 1234, you will have no trouble keeping it in mind, because the numbers are in sequence. If a telephone number ends in 1776 or 1984, you can use natural association, too, since these numbers represent the date of the Declaration of Independence and the title of George Orwell's famous novel. If your automobile license number ends in 1313, you can use the doubled "unlucky" number as a memory aid.

By extending the applications of this natural method, you can remember many numbers you may now be forgetting. For example, a number like 7531357 looks hard, but it can be remembered easily by noting its decreasing, then increasing sequence of odd numbers. Less common dates than 1776 or 1984 may come to your assistance. Probably you know what happened in 1607, 1865, 1918, 1941, and so on. By associating these events with the numbers you wish to remember, you can avoid using a more complex mnemonic system.

Numbers, then, may be easy to remember if they call forth natural associations in your mind. These natural associations can be, and indeed should be, highly personal. Take the number 71430. This number appears to be entirely meaningless; that is, devoid of associations. Yet I know a man who wants to remember this number—it is an insurance account number—and can, because it's his wife's birthday. July 14, 1930, or 7/14/30. For him, the number has natural associations.

You should recognize and use all such numbers that have personal meanings. Your house number, local highway route numbers, meaningful dates—the numbers that don't cause you trouble—can help you immeasurably in memorizing the numbers that do.

YOU MUST WANT TO MEMORIZE

A high school American history teacher tells the story of an average student, David Rouse, who was failing the subject miserably. David couldn't seem to remember dates. In fact, he had no apparent appreciation of what dates meant. They were nonsense to him. In his mind, the years 1812 and 1847 and 1861 and 1898 all merged together as a kind of hazy irrelevancy. David had no desire whatever to learn the chronology of American history.

But David did not have a "poor" memory. Quite the contrary. He had an exceptional memory—when it came to baseball facts and figures. David could remember the batting averages of every major league ballplayer from Hank Aaron to Don Zimmer. He knew Babe Ruth's lifetime record from beginning to end. He also knew Mark McGuire's, Don Mattingly's and Daryl Strawberry's. He had what psychologists call an "eidetic" memory, one in which there exist unusually clear and vivid mental images. David didn't lack the ability to memorize dates in history; he lacked the motivation.

David Rouse never did pass American history. He never tried to pass. Today he works as an unskilled laborer in a factory that makes prefabricated homes. He still amazes his friend with knowledge of baseball statistics. And his friends think he should have gone to college. Well. . .

Sometimes, of course, motivation in a certain area can work for, rather than against, academic success. Jerry Sanford claims that when he was ten years old he learned in order the presidents of the United States. He was an avid stamp collector at the time, and the Presidential series of 1938 has just appeared.The one-cent stamp pictured George Washington, the two-cent stamp John Adams, the three-cent stamp Thomas Jefferson. And so it went, right on through the 22-cent stamp and Grover Cleveland. If a teacher asked for the name of the fourteenth president, Jerry would see a mental image of a dark blue stamp, the number 14 and a picture of Franklin Pierce. He never missed. And he says that his knowledge of presidential chronology helped him even in college. He always had a president to whom he could tie an otherwise isolated event

One page in a stamp album was his constant reference point in American history.

Notice that motivation worked perfectly for both David Rouse and Jerry Sanford. David memorized baseball statistics because he wanted to, and Jerry memorized the appearance of postage stamps because he wanted to. But the motivation in David's case did not help him in school, whereas in Jerry's case it did.

There are several morals to be drawn from these two stories:

1. You *cannot* remember unless you *want* to remember. You must have a strong personal motive if memorization is to occur.

2. You *can* remember what you want to remember. This is true even if the memorization is fairly complicated and extensive.

3. You *should* direct your memorization toward useful goals. That is, you should remember what is worth remembering (and forget the Manhattan telephone directory).

DON'T WASTE YOUR EFFORTS

No matter how bad you may think your memory is, there are a great many numbers you *do* know. Some of these have already been mentioned, and there are many others.

You remember numbers that you use every day. Even the dullest army recruits soon learn their serial numbers, which is by no means easy to do. The number ordinarily has eight nonsequential digits. On top of this, recruits almost immediately learn the serial numbers of their rifle, another tough number. They learn both of these quickly, and they also remember them vividly. They have to. They use the numbers every day of their army life.

Similarly, if you phone the same person every day, you will soon learn and easily remember her number. Even if the number is a difficult one involving an area code—say, 607–734–8529—you will remember it if you use it often enough. The most important numbers in your life, in other words, are numbers that you do *not* forget. You repeat them so often that you memorize them automatically. You do not need an artificial memory system to help you with them. You memorize them by repetition.

When you begin working on the peg method, you should keep these facts in mind. There is no good reason to waste your efforts on numbers you already know, however long and difficult the numbers may be. The only numbers worth using the peg method on are these: (1) long numbers that are important to you but that you do not often use, for example, your bank account number; (2) numbers that are important to your on-the-job success, for example, dates to a history teacher, and (3) numbers that can lessen thumbing through books and catalogs, for example, stock part numbers to a salesperson, plant manager, or snop foreman.

WHAT IS THE PEG METHOD?

The peg method is a system for changing hard-to-remember *numbers* into easy-to-remember *words*. Despite much advertising to the contrary, it is not a modern breakthrough in human thought. The staid old *Encyclopaedia Britannica* traces it back to Stanislaus Mink von Wenussheim, who introduced this "most fertile secret" to the world in 1648. And the basic idea, using letters to represent numbers, goes back even farther. It was first explained in a book by the German poet Konrad Celtes in 1492—an easy date to remember.

Celtes's innovation and von Wenussheim's "fertile secret" were solidly built on the earlier work of Greek and Roman sophists and philosophers. It has been recognized for a long time that numbers are harder to remember than words. Numbers are always abstract, while words are often concrete. Words call up visual images (think of *cat* and in a way you "see" a cat). Numbers do not call up visual images (think of *71* and you probably "see" nothing).

That is the rationale of all modern memory systems. When you use the peg method, the number 71 becomes the word *cat*. To anyone who has studied Dr. Bruno Furst's *Stop Forgetting* (New York: Doubleday, 1979) or any of a host of similar books, the number 71 translates immediately into *cat*; the word *cat* translates into the number 71.

Your first reaction may be, "So what?" After all, the number 71 is not very hard to remember. That's quite true. But you can do a lot more with the peg method than work with two- and three-digit numbers. Take the sentence "A cat runs into the field." That easy-to-remember sentence can translate into a formidable number: 71420211851. And *that*, you will admit, would be a pretty hard number to remember without some sort of memory system.

The peg method is an artificial way of making numbers into words, and vice versa. It requires some initial memorization. You must learn the set of consonants, or "pegs" that will be used in place of numbers.

THE FIRST TEN PEGS

All present-day memory systems are consonants rather than vowels for pegs. There is a good reason for this. If each peg from 0 to 9 can be a consonant, the five vowels can then be placed between them to form words. For example, if the consonant M represents 3 and the consonant R represents 4, it is simple to make a word representing 34. The word can be MARE or MIRE or AMOUR or OMAR or . . .The possibilities are extensive.

Most memory courses explain the logic behind the particular pegs chosen. Thus, N represents 2 because there are two downward strokes in the letter N, and M represents 3 because of the three downward strokes in M. But regardless of the logic involved, you will still have to learn the pegs. Happily, they are not very difficult.

With the peg method, as it is represented in this book, you will find the pegs exceptionally easy. For I have simplified the system to its bare bones, giving each number (except 7) only one peg.

Here are the pegs:

1—T
2—N
3—M
4—R
5—L
6—SH

7—K (or "hard" C; e.g., Corn)

8—F

9—B

0—S

    You will next have to create words and mental pictures for each number you wish to remember. Therefore, you will need a key word for each of the basic numbers. You could easily devise these key words yourself, but here are ten that should prove satisfactory:

    1—(T)—Tie (picture a necktie)

    2—(N)—Noah (picture the man and his ark)

    3—(M)—Me (picture yourself)

    4—(R)—Ray (picture a ray of light)

    5—(L)—Lee (picture the Southern general)

    6—(SH)—SHow (picture a Broadway musical)

    7—(K)—Key (picture a door key)

    8—(F)—Fee (picture a dollar bill)

    9—(B)—Boy (picture a barefoot boy)

    0—(S)—Saw (picture a buzz saw)

    Whether you accept these key words or make up a list of your own, you cannot simply file them and forget them. You must memorize them and then practice counting with them. Until you have the peg code memorized perfectly, you will not be able to go on to more difficult problems.

    The ten key words above are helpful in remembering the peg code itself. They are also useful as mnemonic devices in their own right. If you need to remember 962, for instance, you can picture a Boy going to a SHow in which Noah is the leading character. Thus, Boy (9) plus SHow (6) plus Noah (2) gives you 962. But trying to apply this method to five- and six-digit numbers is likely to be futile.

    Since this is so, you will have to make up your own key words, phrases, or sentences for most numbers. Ordinarily the numbers you wish to remember will be long and difficult ones. To master these numbers, you will proceed on a personal basis. You will construct your own words, phrases, and sentences, using the basic peg letters to represent the numbers. Here's how it's done.

HOW TO MAKE YOUR OWN KEYS

Suppose your social security number is 071–02–3481. How can you translate this number into an easy-to-remember word, phrase, or sentence? First, write down the pegs you will use. 0 is S, 7 is K (or hard C), 1 is T, and so on. You will write these down in order:

SKT–SN–MRFT

So far it looks like gibberish. But watch. The first three letters will make SKIT with only a single vowel added. Once you have accepted SKIT, you can proceed from there. Why not put a verb in the second group of letters? SKIT–IS ON will give you the first six digits. In the last group of letters, RFT looks very much like RAFT. That leaves only the M to take care of. And it's easy: MY. Thus you get:

SKIT–IS ON–MY RAFT
07 1–0   2–3   4 81

Now let's try a couple of telephone numbers. Take 942–6740. The number works out in the peg code to BRN–SHKRS, which can easily be made into BARN SHAKERS (or BORN SHAKERS or BURN SHAKERS). Fixing the proper image in your mind will allow you to remember the telephone number forever.

Next try the number 731–8502. This number becomes CMT–FLSN. Very easy. COMET FLIES ON.

You will discover that this method works best if you count double consonants as single numbers. Thus, BARREL translates as 945, not as 9445. Flexibility demands this rule. Many English words have double consonants, and these words would be almost unusable if each consonant were to represent a number. Under the rule, therefore, ROLLER and RULER are both the same number: 454.

USING FIRST LETTERS AS KEYS

Sometimes a long number will not translate satisfactorily into a word, phrase, or short sentence. The telephone number 977–0780, for example, does not work very well. In the peg code it comes out as BKK-SKFS. The last four letters will easily make SKIFFS. But what can you do with the first three letters? BKK will not make a common word.

When this happens, you can make a sentence in which *only the first letters of the words are used as pegs.* This method allows great latitude in constructing key sentences. You can fit each sentence to the person with whom the number is connected. For instance, suppose the telephone number 977–0780 belongs to William Courtney, the owner of a kennel. You can fit the telephone number to the man quite easily: "Bill Courtney Can't Say 'Cats For Sale.' " By using the first letter of each word, you get BCC–SCFS. All the Cs are hard, or Ks, and the number comes out 977–0780. Of course, to have the method work, you must remember the sentence exactly.

The main drawback to this method is the length of the key sentences. However, this disadvantage is lessened somewhat by the fact that the sentences lead to "natural" associations.

Is the system worth the effort it takes? There are many people who think it is.

HOW ARNOLD FRYE USES THE PEG METHOD

Arnold Frye runs a small wholesale dry goods store. He uses the telephone perhaps 12 to 15 times each day. During an average week he talks to about 40 different people. Since these 40 people are his regular customers, there are obvious advantages in being able to remember all of their telephone numbers.

Arnold remembers every number by using the peg method. Most of the numbers require key sentences or phrases. He has one phone number, however, with an unusual single-word key. The number is 943-0120, and the word is BRIMSTONES. "it's a perfect key," says Arnold, "because the guy at 943–0120 is a regular devil!"

THE PEG METHOD FOR REMEMBERING DATES

Most high school students are like David Rouse. They hate to memorize dates in history. What the students may not realize is that their teachers usually don't like dates either. But it's just about impossible to teach history without knowing a great many dates. A history teacher who has a perfect, semiautomatic mastery of dates therefore has a real advantage. She no longer needs to worry about the inauguration date of William McKinley, the year of the "Tariff of Abominations," or the date of the Treaty of Ghent. She has the key that will give her each answer. Consequently, she can use her energies to concentrate on more important matters.

One history teacher I know uses the peg method to keep dates straight. Here is the set of keys he has devised to remember the dates of America's participation in major wars. (Notice that he has keyed only the last two digits of each date.)

		7	5	8	3
American Revolution	1775–1783	Can	Liberty	Free	Men?
		1	2	1	4
War of 1812	1812–1814	The Navy was	The	Rescuer	
		4	6	4	
Mexican War	1846–1847	Rightfully	we SHould	Resist	
		7			
		Conquest			
		6	1	6	5
Civil War	1861–1865	a SHame	They	SHot	Lincoln
		9	8		
Spanish–American War	1898	Bold	Folly		
		1	7	1	8
First World War	1917–1918	Trenches	Came	To	Front
		4	1	4	5
Second World War	1941–1945	Russia	Thinks	we Really	Lost
		5	0	5	3
Korean War	1950–1953	Line	Smashed,	Lost	MacArthur

A FINAL WORD

Well, that's the peg method. If you are serious about using it, you must work with it every day. Working with it now and then will not do. Just as a pianist becomes more sure of his musical technique with each practice session, you too can improve your memory technique only through concentration, training, and effort.

Mnemonic devices like the peg method have a rightful place in the mental storehouse of a power thinker. They are something that can be of real value if they are sensibly and sparingly used, but they are not the last word in mental dynamics. They have limitations which are pretty apparent.

They also have a surface glitter that can lead a person to use them when they are not appropriate. In this connection, you will do well to heed the warning of Alex Osborn—the creative genius of Batten, Barton, Durtine and Osborn—when he says "No memory expert can have at hand any greater 'knowledge' than a moron armed with a *World Almanac.*"

TEN TIPS FOR REMEMBERING NUMBERS

1. Whenever possible, use "natural" associations to remember numbers. Well-known dates and sequential figures provide natural associations.

2. Bear in mind that you cannot remember something unless you want to remember it. Motivation is vital.

3. Direct your memorization toward useful goals. Don't bother trying to memorize the numbers in your local telephone book, or anything else silly.

4. Don't use a memory system on numbers you use every day, even if these are long and difficult numbers. It's not necessary.

5. Use the peg method for numbers that you need to know but cannot remember without an artificial aid.

6. Learn the ten basic pegs: 1 is *T*, 2 is *N*, 3 is *M*, 4, is *R*, 5 is *L*, 6 is *SH*, 7 is *K* (or *C*), 8 is *F*, 9 is *B*, 0 is *S*.

7. Practice counting with key words for the basic numbers: 1 is Tie, 2 is Noah, 3 is Me, 4 is Ray, 5 is Lee, 6 is SHow, 7 is Key, 8 is Fee, 9 is Boy, 0 is Saw.

8. Make up your own key words, phrases, and sentences for long numbers that you wish to remember.

9. If a long number will not translate easily into a word, phrase, or short sentence, devise a sentence in which only the first letters of the words are pegs.

10. Practice often with the peg code and with the key words, phrases, and sentences you have constructed.

Chapter 9

Practical Ways to Build Your Vocabulary

- Increasing Your Stockpile of Words
- Reading—the Sine Qua Non
- Broaden the Range of Your Experiences
- Conversation as a Vocabulary Builder
- Words and Their Pedigree
- The Key to 100,000 Words
- Don't be Afraid to Say "Lugubrious"
- Vocabulary Quizzes for Fun and Profit
- Your Dictionary Has the Answers
- Ten Tips for Vocabulary Building

If a psychologist were asked to estimate your chances for success, what would she first want to know about you? Your family background? Your educational record? Your personality traits? No. The first thing she would want to know is the extent of your vocabulary.

Psychologists have found that the extent of a person's vocabulary is the most important single factor correlating with success—not just scholastic success, mind you, but success on the job as well.

Surveys by Johnson O'Connor's Human Engineering Laboratory, an aptitude testing institution located in eight United States cities, Mexico, and Canada, indicate that a superior vocabulary is more likely to accompany occupational success than any other measurable trait.

When O'Connor gave vocabulary tests to executive and supervisory personnel in 39 large industrial plants, he obtained eye-opening results. Out of a possible total of 272 points, the following average scores were achieved:

Presidents and vice-presidents 236

Managers 168

Superintendents 140

Foremen 114

Floor Bosses 86

Top business executives actually outscored college and university professors by a narrow margin.

Surely, it is no accident that in almost every case the extent of a person's vocabulary correlated with career level and income.

In view of this, it seems absurd that the average American

adult, through lack of effort, adds only about 50 new words a year to his or her vocabulary. Why is it that vocabulary building often ends, for all practical purposes, after high school or college? There are reasons for it, of course—all of them bad. Adults are just as capable of learning new words as children, and they have a real professional and social stake in doing so.

INCREASING YOUR STOCKPILE OF WORDS

An average 14-year-old child has a vocabulary of about 10,000 words, an average high school graduate 15,000, and an average college graduate between 20,000 and 30,000. Formal schooling is a potent vocabulary builder. The educational process forces students to learn unfamiliar words. New ideas require new terminology, and textbooks become progressively "harder."

Once a person graduates from school, however, he can choose his own reading matter, and this is when sloth frequently sets in. When this happens, most people, including college graduates, still have an inadequate command of words. They grope for words, use inexact words, and express complex thoughts poorly. They are embarrassed by their limitations, yet they seldom make any real effort to alter the situation. But those few who do make the effort are well rewarded, and you should be among them.

How can you improve the range and depth of your vocabulary? There are many ways. You can choose reading material that challenges your present vocabulary. You can widen the scope of your experiences, learning useful new words along the way. You can listen to people whose vocabularies are better than your own.

In addition, you can cultivate an interest in words, learning about prefixes, roots, suffixes, and origins of words. You can test yourself with many kinds of vocabulary quizzes. You can become adept at using that indispensable arsenal of words, the dictionary.

Yes, there are numerous ways to build a stronger vocabulary. You should know them all; each one is worth serious study and sustained use.

READING—THE SINE QUA NON

Much of your present vocabulary owes its existence to your past reading. Now, it is perfectly true that you learned your first few thousand words not by reading, but by listening, pointing, asking questions, and repeating answers. You acquired this vocabulary mostly from your parents and older brothers and sisters. The words you learned were primarily *concrete* ones: *mother, baby, shoe, dog.*

Then a wonderful change occurred in your vocabulary building—you started reading. As soon as you began to read, you found yourself coming across unfamiliar words constantly, words you had never seen or heard or noticed before. Quite a few of these words were *abstract* ones, and you had no idea at all of what they meant. You didn't look up these words in the dictionary, even after you knew how to use it . . . but you learned the words nevertheless. How? By observing the words over and over again, and by seeing only a vague idea of what these new words meant. Later, when you had seen them many times, often with implied definitions, you had a more exact concept of their meaning. Today, when you see words like *responsibility, violent,* or *imaginative,* you can easily give approximate dictionary definitions of them.

Yet in all likelihood no one ever defined these words for you. You never checked their meanings in a dictionary. You did not learn them from vocabulary quizzes. Instead, you learned them from reading, with important help, perhaps, from hearing them used orally—and you learned them without even realizing you were doing so!

Let's look now at some words you may not know. Can you define the words *mountebank, comstockery,* or *polizei?* These are uncommon words in English, and scarcely vital to the average person's vocabulary; but you will have no trouble with *polizei* if you have studied German. However, if you are familiar with the writings of H. L. Mencken—whether you have studied German or not—I'll bet you can define all three words. For these are three of Mencken's favorites. They occur very frequently in his writing. If you are a Mencken reader, you are pretty sure to have a good idea of what they mean whether you have ever looked them up in a dictionary or not. You have acquired the words by exposure to them in print, by seeing them used in context, often with built-in definitions, and you have added them to your recognition vocabulary.

Next . . . Do you know the meanings of the words *glasnost, ozone, software,* or *fractile?* You do if you have been reading the newspapers regularly. Yet just a few years ago these would have been odd and unfamiliar words to most adults in the United States. Reading, once again with an assist from listening, has painlessly and effectively added these words to your vocabulary.

Reading is indeed essential for vocabulary building. And, happily, the reading does not have to be deep, turgid, and tiresome. Many of the most readable modern writers use some words you are not likely to know but ought to add to your vocabulary.

William Safire and William F. Buckley, Jr., are two excellent examples. You may not always agree with what these writers say, but your vocabulary is likely to increase from year to year if you read them.

Chapter 4 stressed the importance of a planned reading program and the necessity of choosing high-quality newspapers, magazines, and books. This advice is worth repeating here. Almost any good writer will occasionally use words you should know but don't, and the only way you can even discover such words is by seeing them in black and white.

"True enough," you say, "but how do I *learn* these words?" One suggestion is to underline words you do not know, then guess at their meaning and proceed with your reading. This is good, common-sense advice. There is no point in ruining your enjoyment of a book or article by habitually grabbing the dictionary to check word meanings (and you won't do that anyway, I'm sure!). You can always check the words later if you wish. But whether you actually look up definitions or not, you will be improving your vocabulary almost unconsciously *just by noticing the words.* This may sound like mysticism, but it is not. In fact, it is basically the way you learned thousands of words that are now a part of your vocabulary.

BROADEN THE RANGE OF YOUR EXPERIENCES

One of my close friends is a man of many interests. He is a stamp and coin collector, an amateur minerologist, a baseball and football fan, and a student of local history. He is convinced that these activities are powerful, painless vocabulary builders.

He cites an example. One time, he spent an afternoon in the

Hall of Minerals and Gems at the American Museum of Natural History. He noticed two Cub Scouts working their way from cabinet to cabinet looking at the specimens, and he heard one of them say to the other, "Look here, Pete. Look at the orthoclase."

"How many adults," he asks, "have ever heard the word orthoclase? Very few. Yet orthoclase is as common a word to a rock and mineral collector, even a young one, as blasphemy is to a theologian."

Similarly, how many adults will recognize the words *florin, rupee, piaster, dinar, sen,* and *pfennig?* You probably know some of them. But there are preadolescent coin collectors who know all of them, for each word is the denomination of a foreign coin: *florin* from Great Britain and the Netherlands, *rupee* from India, *piaster* from Turkey and other countries, *dinar* from Iraq, *sen* from Japan, and *pfennig* from Germany.

These examples could be multiplied endlessly, which leads inevitably to this conclusion: The greater your range of interests and activities, the greater your vocabulary. Now, as Maxwell Nurnberg and Morris Rosenblum have stressed in their superb book *How to Build a Better Vocabulary* (New York: Warner Books, 1988), not all the words you learn will be "technical" ones—as the above illustrations unquestionably are. Many will be words that can be used in everyday conversation. A sports fan, for instance, will come across such words as *debacle, juggernaut, indomitable, stymie,* and *redoubtable* just by reading the sports section of the daily newspaper. She can use these the rest of her life.

Yes, you can increase your vocabulary by increasing the range of your interests, activities, and experiences. If you do not have a hobby, you should certainly choose one. It will not only make you a more interesting person, it will aid your vocabulary at the same time. Moreover, it doesn't make much difference what your interest is—tennis; fishing; boating; golf; photography; painting; or collecting antiques, stamps, coins, minerals, old books, or phonograph records—any of these will help you widen the scope of your experiences, meet new people, and add some useful words to your vocabulary.

There is no need to belabor the point. The lesson is clear. By leading a fuller life you can acquire a richer vocabulary—and have a lot of fun in the process!

CONVERSATION AS A VOCABULARY BUILDER

One obvious way to increase the range of your experiences and the extent of your vocabulary is to meet new, interesting, and intelligent people. As Longfellow once said, "A single conversation across the table with a wise man is better than ten years' study of books." It pays to become acquainted with people whose conversations can broaden your horizons, add zest to your life, and introduce you to new worlds of words.

Persons of superior intelligence generally possess superior vocabularies. Therefore, you should go out of your way to meet and talk with as many gifted and informed people as possible. Just as a tennis player does not improve his game by playing inferior opponents, neither does an intelligent person improve his or her vocabulary by talking with people who speak only in monosyllables.

WORDS AND THEIR PEDIGREE

One of the more unusual ways to increase your vocabulary, and acquire a liberal education, too, is to become interested in the origins of words. (Doing this can also help make you a lively conversationalist.)

Let's take as an etymological example the word *thug*. You're familiar with it; you've seen it hundreds of times. Now if you stop to think about it—as most people, of course, never have—you might guess that *thug* was originally an underworld slang expression or a disreputable Anglo-Saxon term. Not so. The word comes from Hindustani. Thugs, in old India, were members of a fanatical religious sect who robbed wealthy travelers and then used part of the loot to honor their goddess Kali. The original thugs were wiped out long ago, but their name lives on.

There are literally thousands of words that have equally interesting origins. Many of these words are in everyday use, like *thug* or *khaki* (which also comes from Hindustani), and will not be new additions to your vocabulary. However, by becoming interested in word origins, you are likely to become more interested in words in general. You will never greatly increase your vocabulary unless you are genuinely interested in words.

Word origins, as previously mentioned, make fascinating and practical conversation pieces. Take the origin of the word *spoonerism*. A spoonerism is the accidental transposing of the first letters of words or phrases. The word comes from the name of the Reverend William A. Spooner (1844–1930), warden of New College, Oxford, who had the habit of making such mistakes. When Spooner tried to say "a well-oiled bicycle," for instance, it came out "a well-boiled icicle." "A crushing blow" was "a blushing crow." One of the classic modern spoonerisms is a misguided radio announcer's advice to "reach for the breast in bed"—rather than "the best in bread."

Your dictionary, if it is an unabridged or college edition, will explain the derivations of words. There are also books that discuss word origins in some detail.

Now, you may be like the man who swore he "would rather have an inch of dog than a mile of pedigree," and feel that the meanings of words and not their origins are your main concern. To some extent you are right. However, if you want to increase your vocabulary, you *must* become interested in words—and learning about word origins is one of the best ways to do it.

THE KEY TO 100,000 WORDS

Prefixes, roots, and suffixes are the raw material of the English language. They are the stuff of which words are made. A knowledge of prefixes, roots, and suffixes allows any reasonably intelligent person to make a stab at defining a word like *antidisestablishmentarianism* in spite of its formidable appearance, or to define a word like *antimalarial* without a moment's hesitation.

An eighth grade English teacher tells this story about teaching prefixes, suffixes, and word roots to one of her classes on the day after Ernest Hemingway's death. While she was explaining the meanings of *mono-*, *bi-*, *tri-*, and *quadri-*, a boy raised his hand and asked what *sui-* meant, as in *suicide*. Now, as is so often the case, there was little connection between *sui-* and the prefixes being taught; but being a good Latin scholar and wishing to answer all questions, the teacher replied that *sui-* meant "of oneself." Not being able to think of any other example except suicide—in fact, there is no common one—she continued with that. *Sui-*, "of oneself"; *-cide*, "a killing." Thus, *suicide* is "a killing of oneself."

So far, so good. But of course it didn't end there. *Insecticide* entered the picture from another student. *Insect*, the teacher patiently explained, is a word known to everyone. *Insecticide* is "an insect killer."

And so it went. Before the period was over, the class had learned about homicide, genocide, parricide, infanticide, matricide, patricide, fraticide, sororicide, and uxoicide.

For days the teacher trembled lest some parent come storming into the school asking what in the devil was being taught teenagers nowadays. It never happened. The teacher herself is now persuaded that there was probably no more powerful way to teach these prefixes than to combine them with the sanguinary root *-cide*. Months later, she reports, most of the students in the class had a pretty good idea of the meanings of such words as *matriarchy*, *patrimony*, *fraternal*, and *uxorial*—not easy words, you will admit, for eighth graders who have not studied Latin. Fortunately, the students had been given the keys to unlock their meanings.

Prefixes, roots, and suffixes are truly the keys to a staggering number of English words. Leonard A. Stevens, a writer on this subject, claims that 14 words with their prefixes and roots provide the necessary tools for figuring out the meanings of no fewer than *100,000* words, four times the average person's vocabulary (see pages 120–121). Although this claim should be taken with a grain of salt—for prefixes and roots will not give you exact definitions and can sometimes lead you astray—the fact remains that knowing prefixes, roots, and suffixes is almost as valuable to the vocabulary builder as the lever was to Archimedes. "Give me a large enough lever," said the brilliant Greek, "and I can move the earth." Prefixes, roots, and suffixes are a gigantic lever to the vocabulary builder.

DON'T BE AFRAID TO SAY "LUGUBRIOUS" ═══════

Once you have acquired a new word, you must not be afraid to use it. Don't be afraid to say *lugubrious*. Don't be afraid to say *jejune*. Don't be afraid to say *anthropomorphic*. In fact, don't be afraid to say *any* word—if you know what it means and if it fits the situation. For unless you say it, you will forget it.

Your recognition vocabulary and your writing vocabulary, like everyone else's, are much larger than your speaking vocabulary. You know the meanings of many words you never use when speaking. You even use many words correctly in writing that you never use in speaking. Why? Because you are self-conscious about using "big" words; and because, when you are speaking, you can't always think of exactly the right word at exactly the right time.

The one right word used at precisely the right time can create a tremendously favorable impression, and it won't cause jeers among your listeners. If anything, it will cause cheers.

I once heard a native of upstate New York, describing her recent trip to California. When asked what she thought of the people in the Los Angeles area, she replied, "Oh, I suppose they're not much different from us in the East; but in a way they do seem, well, a little meretricious."

My opinion of the woman went up considerably. So did that of another person who was listening to her. No sooner had she finished the sentence than he said: "Miss Brody, that word is *perfect*. 'Meretricious' describes them to a 'T.' "

You may not agree with Miss Brody that Southern Californians are meretricious. But you will have to agree that she picked a superb word to describe her impression of them.

You must not be self-conscious about using words you have just added to your vocabulary. For one thing, you will remember the words better if you immediately begin using them in conversation. And you will have them ready for use in the future—when one of them may be the "perfect word."

One vocabulary expert maintains that the only way you will remember new words is by using three or four times in a single day after learning them. This is a good habit to cultivate, for repetition is the key to retention. Why not try it? The next time you learn a new word, try to work it into your conversation three times during the course of that day.

Try following the example of the little boy in the cartoon who says to his mother, "We learned a new word in school today. Try and surmise what it is. I'll give you three surmises." My surmise is that it was *surmise*. And I'll bet (or surmise) the boy will remember *surmise* forever!

KEY TO 100,000 WORDS*

	PREFIX	ITS OTHER SPELLINGS	ITS MEANING	MASTER WORDS	ROOT	ITS OTHER SPELLINGS	ITS MEANING
1	DE-	—	Down or Away	DETAIN	TAIN	Ten, Tin	To Have or Hold
2	INTER-	—	Between	INTERMITTENT	MITT	Miss, Mis, Mit	To Send
3	PRE-	—	Before	PRECEPT	CEPT	Cap, Capt, Ceiv, Ceit, Cip	To Take or Seize
4	OB-	Oc- Of- Op-	To, Toward, Against	OFFER	FER	Lat, Lay	To Bear or Carry
5	IN-	Il- Im- Ir-	Into	INSIST	SIST	Sta	To Stand, Endure, or Persist
6	MONO-	—	One or Alone	MONOGRAPH	GRAPH	—	To Write
7	EPI-	—	Over, Upon, or Beside	EPILOGUE	LOG	Ology	Speech or Science
8	AD-	A- Ac- Ag- Al- An- Ap- Ar- As- At-	To or Toward	ASPECT	SPECT	Spec, Spi, Spy	To Look

#	Prefix	Variants	Meaning	Word	Root	Root forms	Root meaning
9	UN-	—	Not	UNCOMPLICATED	PLIC	Play, Plex, Ploy, Ply	To Fold, Bend, Twist, or Interweave
	COM-	Co- Col- Con- Cor-	With or Together				
10	NON-	—	Not	NONEXTENDED	TEND	Tens, Tent	To Stretch
	EX-	E- Ef-	Out or Formerly				
11	RE-	—	Back or Again	REPRODUCTION	DUCT	Duc, Duit, Duk	To Lead, Make, Shape, or Fashion
	PRO-	—	Forward or In favor of				
12	IN-	Il- Im- Ir-	Not	INDISPOSED	POS	Pound, Pon, Post	To Put or Place
	DIS-	Di- Dif-	Apart from				
13	OVER-	—	Above	OVERSUFFICIENT	FIC	Fac, Fact, Fash, Feat	To Make or Do
	SUB-	Suc- Suf- Sug- Sup- Sur- Sus-	Under				
14	MIS-	—	Wrong or Wrongly	MISTRANSCRIBE	SCRIBE	Scrip, Scriv	To Write
	TRANS-	Tra- Tran-	Across or Beyond				

*Reprinted by permission of James I. Brown, University of Minnesota.

VOCABULARY QUIZZES FOR FUN
AND PROFIT

The best way to acquire new words is the easiest and most natural way—by wide reading, new experiences, and stimulating conversation. But the natural way is not the only way; there are a number of somewhat artificial means for improving your vocabulary, which, properly used, can be quite helpful. You are familiar with most of them. They include printed quizzes, word games, dictionary study, and books on vocabulary building. These are worth exploring, although anyone who puts his or her whole trust in such devices is doomed to disappointment.

By far the most popular of the artificial methods of vocabulary building is the printed quiz. The printed quiz seems to be a magazine publisher's delight. Scores of popular magazines have employed it at one time or another, and the largest selling magazine in the world, *The Reader's Digest,* has printed a vocabulary quiz every month for many years. There is probably not a literate adult in the United States who has not tried to solve at least once "It Pays to Increase Your Word Power." This is a useful quiz, for it contains words you really should know but may not.

Most people, I'm sure, take the quiz in a spare moment, then forget it. They also forget the words they have just "learned," which is the primary fault of all artificial vocabulary building devices. However, it is entirely possible to take this quiz, mark the words you have missed, cut the page out of the magazine and save it, along with future quizzes, in a file folder. Then occasionally you can go back and retest yourself on the tough words. If you miss them again, make a special effort to use the words in your conversation. In other words, learn them! Don't just toy with them. Retest yourself on them until you are absolutely certain you know their meaning. This is the only way "It Pays to Increase Your Word Power" and similar quizzes can be made into anything more than mildly diverting games.

Another kind of vocabulary building is an impromptu, person-to-person, question-and-answer game, in which your wife, husband, or a friend thumbs through a good dictionary and asks you to define words *you have both probably heard.* This demands a certain amount of common sense in selection, as well as participants of approximately equal intelligence and interests. There is little point in having a botanist ask her husband to define *tetrasporangium*, or having an artist ask his wife to identify the word for some obscure process for preparing a canvas for painting.

Nonetheless, sensibly conducted, this kind of vocabulary quiz can be quite purposeful—far more so than, say, Scrabble, which has no real educational value at all. For one thing, the game will focus attention on words that are in fairly common use, but whose meanings are hazy in your mind. Perhaps, though, it will tend to make you a dictionary user.

YOUR DICTIONARY HAS THE ANSWERS

A librarian in the Rochester, New York, Public Library once told me that she doubts whether one person in 20 who uses the library knows how to get maximum benefit out of a good dictionary. This seems amazing. It indicates that even people who recognize the value of reading do not always recognize the importance of the dictionary. As a matter of fact, I know a prominent local businessman and a highly regarded lawyer who do not even have desk dictionaries in their homes. Yet they are both acutely aware of the need for a broad, striking vocabulary—a paradox worth pondering!

What will a good dictionary tell you about a word? It will give you one or more definitions of words you have to look up, obviously something a literate person ought to be able to get without writing away to his or her newspaper's syndicated vocabulary expert. And it will give you much, much more. It will give you correct spellings, possible alternate spellings, synonyms, antonyms, parts of speech, and word origins. If you will take the time to read the introductory material in a good desk dictionary (probably the most unused part of any dictionary), you will be amazed to discover the amount of useful information your dictionary actually contains.

There are many good desk dictionaries available including *Webster's Ninth New Collegiate Dictionary*, 9th edition (Springfield, MA: Merriam-Webster, Inc., 1989) or *Webster's New World Dictionary of the American Language*, 3d College Edition (New York: Simon & Schuster, 1988). The money spent on a dictionary can be the best investment you have ever made.

One word of warning: Don't buy a paperback dictionary. There is no such thing as a good one, and there probably never will be. A first-rate dictionary must be a big book, and it must be one that will hold up under daily use. As the most valuable single tool for a person who wants to improve his or her mind, a first rate clothbound desk dictionary is the greatest book bargain in the world.

TEN TIPS FOR VOCABULARY BUILDING

1. Choose challenging reading material. You can't learn new words until you encounter them.
2. Notice every new word you come across in your reading or listening.
3. Broaden the scope of your experiences. Meet people with different interests—and different vocabularies—from your own.
4. Converse with people who have better vocabularies than you have.
5. Take a genuine interest in the origins of words. Learn how to uncover word origins.
6. Pay close attention to prefixes, roots, and suffixes of words. Discover what they mean.
7. When you learn a new word, try to use it in your conversation at least three times that day.
8. Become acquainted with printed vocabulary quizzes, both in magazines and books.
9. Devise and use impromptu vocabulary quizzes.
10. Buy a good desk dictionary and learn how to use it to fullest advantage.

Part 3

The Dynamics of Critical and Creative Thought

Knowledge, in truth, is the
great sun in the firmament.
Life and power are scattered
with all its beams.

—DANIEL WEBSTER

Chapter 10 ══════════

The Elements of Logical Thinking

"CONTRARIWISE," CONTINUED TWEEDLEDEE , "if it was so, it might be; and if it were so, it would be; but as it isn't, it ain't. That's logic."

Is it? There are people who would define logic in about the same way as Tweedledee in Lewis Carroll's *Through the Looking-Glass*. These people consider logic to be either pompous nonsense or else a verbal trick—something to bedevil schoolchildren with, but nothing to use in dealing with practical affairs. Unfortunately, this distrust of logic is not confined to uneducated people. Stanley Baldwin, a former Prime Minister of Great Britain, once said:

> It seems to me that one of the reasons why our people are alive and flourishing, and have avoided many of the troubles that have fallen to less happy nations, is because we have never been guided by logic in anything we have done.

That is an amazing statement. Had Stanley Baldwin himself "never been guided by logic" in anything he did, he probably would not have been alive and flourishing at all. He might have walked blithely into the path of a train when he was a child. Or he might have locked himself in an icebox on a warm day in July. Or he might have jumped out a tenth-story window to see if he could fly.

It is safe to say that everyone is guided, to some extent, by logic in everything she does. For instance, no one knowingly contradicts herself. If you were to say, "Yes, I think all General Motors cars are the best on the road, but I think the Chevrolet is the worst car ever built," most listeners would regard you as addlebrained. They would recognize your statement as illogical, though they would not be likely to call it a "fallacy of formal logic," which it is.

Logic, used or misused, is a vital part of your life and work. You can no more avoid it than you can avoid language itself. For logic is a function of language, and unless you know something about it, your thoughts, words, and actions will suffer the consequences. A person who knows what logic is and knows how to use it has a priceless tool to use in her dealings with people, ideas, and events.

WHAT IS LOGIC?

Logic can be defined simply as the process of asking intelligent questions and trying to find answers to them.

Suppose you are a teacher who has been asked to recommend a textbook for use in the coming year. You would not dash down to the local bookstore, since you know it does not sell textbooks. Nor would you write the sales department of just one major publisher and ask for their advice. Probably you would not recommend the first textbook you saw, either.

Instead, you would devise a plan that would give you a *rational* answer to the question: "What textbook should I recommend?" you would try to get copies of the major textbooks in print. Then you would examine each of them carefully. You would compare and contrast. You would weigh good features against bad features, eliminating some books in the process. Eventually you would have two or three books, clearly superior to the rest, from which to choose. You would then evaluate the texts again, and finally you would reach an informed decision.

Now, *that's* logic. In fact, the process just described involves a combination of the two forms of formal logic: inductive reasoning and deductive reasoning. Both of these forms are worth looking at in some detail.

HOW INDUCTIVE REASONING WORKS

Perhaps you believe that teenagers are erratic drivers. How did you arrive at this belief? Well, you may have heard it from friends and relatives. You may have read it in a newspaper or magazine. Or you may have observed a number of teenage drivers, noticing one making a right turn from the left-hand lane of traffic, another stopping suddenly in the middle of the roadway, another signaling for a turn he or she did not make, and still another talking to a friend rather than looking at the road.

From all of these sources, you reached a conclusion: "Teenagers are erratic drivers." This generalization was arrived at by the process of inductive reasoning. You listened, you read, and you also observed teenage drivers (though not very objectively perhaps). From your experience you decided that teenage drivers are erratic and must be watched warily.

This process of gathering evidence and reaching a conclusion is one kind of inductive reasoning. There is another kind. Suppose you decide to examine a belief to see whether it is valid. Again, teenage drivers can be used as an illustration. Instead of observing and later generalizing from your observations, you might say, "For *the sake of argument*, I'll assume that teenagers are erratic drivers." After making this hypothesis, you then begin listening, reading, and observing to determine whether or not teenagers really do drive erratically. Eventually you reach a conclusion as to whether your hypothesis is right or wrong.

The first form of inductive reasoning, then, is the accumulation of evidence; the second is the testing of a hypothesis. Both forms are useful, and both are extremely common—not only in the writing of research papers or in the conduct of laboratory experiments, but in everyday social and business life.

THE POWER OF INDUCTIVE REASONING

One of the most successful men I know literally lives by his wits—or, more accurately, by his ability to reason inductively. He is a man in his forties who lives in Philadelphia, a man who contrived to retire, you might say, at the age of twenty-nine. He earns a six-figure yearly income, and this income has increased every year for the past fifteen years.

Here's how it happened. After college he entered a brokerage firm as a trainee. He learned everything he could about stock market investment and speculation. He watched people playing the market and learned exactly how it could be done profitably. After eight years he left the firm, adjourned to his home, and began his own modest stock market operations. He followed the same basic advice of all armchair speculators: "Buy low. Sell high." But he actually managed to do it.

Now the stock market is more than just rows of names and figures in the daily paper. It is a living, breathing organism. Every one of those names represents a corporation: people, products, sales, profit-and-loss. If you know—really *know*—the stories behind those names and figures, you know something that the average investor simply does not know. You know where certain companies are going, and why. You know which stocks are good buys at the selling prices and which are bad. You know whether a company is striking pay dirt, panning fools' gold, or looking in vain for the Lost Dutchman mine.

But knowing all this takes work. It takes many hours of gathering evidence about industries and specific companies, sifting this evidence, and drawing valid conclusions from it. All this requires inductive reasoning of a high order. At the outset my friend in Philadelphia had only two choices: he could be right, or he could be broke. Over the years he has been right more often than not. He owes his financial independence to inductive reasoning; that is, to his ability to gather evidence and reach sound conclusions.

The first vital step, then, is gathering evidence. This step is performed by everyone, everyday, but few people do it consciously. My friend in Philadelphia does—and so should you.

GATHERING EVIDENCE

When a company wants to market a new product, it gathers all the information it can about what will appeal to the public. It doesn't do this by guesswork. It collects evidence from every possible source. It uses market research to the hilt. Only after it has done so does it feel justified in concluding, "People will buy this product."

The need for gathering evidence before mass marketing begins is well illustrated by the classic case of the chicken frankfurters. Some entrepreneurs at Cornell University, having fashioned a hot dog made of chicken, decided to test it under two names at a local grocery store. The first name was a prosaic one: "Chicken Franks." The second was more jazzy: "Bird Dogs." Every single person involved in "research and development" was convinced that the Bird Dogs would run away, metaphorically speaking, from the Chicken Franks. But no. Consumers wanted no part of

Bird Dogs, and the Chicken Franks, displayed right beside them on the counter, outsold Bird Dogs by a wide margin. Had the Cornellians boldly guessed on Bird Dogs, they would have been dead wrong.

The Bird Dog caper has a moral. If you merely *assume* that you are right about your beliefs, without ever testing them, you are making a serious mistake. There may be something in a mysterious "sixth sense," but it is not very much. Generally, the power thinker is the one who subjects *all* of his or her ideas to careful analysis.

GUIDELINES FOR INDUCTIVE REASONING

When faced with a problem, gather all the evidence you can about it. Don't rationalize, but, on the other hand, don't tacitly assume that you know the answer. Work it out for yourself. The method you use will vary each time, but there are certain guidelines to follow:

1. Beware of making generalizations that contain the words *all, always,* and *never.* All doctors are rich (false). Politicians are *always* crooked (false). Broad generalizations are *never* true. (Work that one out carefully!)

2. Remember that statistics can lie. Richard D. Altick in his book *Preface to Critical Reading,* 6th edition (New York: Holt, Rinehart and Winston, 6th edition, 1984) makes the point very well. In a civil service examination, he says, the scores were 95, 92, 90, 88, 84, 84, 84, 84, 83, 80, 76, 76, 75, 70, 69, 60, 58, 53, 50, 42, and 40. The *arithmetical mean* is 73. The *simple mean* is 67.5. The *median* is 76. The *mode* is 84. Take your pick. That's what advertisers, politicians, columnists, and special pleaders of all sorts very often do.

3. Don't be fooled by the words *average* and *typical.* There is no such thing as an "average" or "typical" anything. An example of why you should be wary of these words: A student once complained to her teacher, a professor of philosophy: "I was down at Grand Central Station this morning, and I saw a herd of commuters get off the train

from Summit. What a faceless, soulless, conformist mass!" To which the professor replied: "I get off that train every morning!"

TEST YOUR HYPOTHESIS

Sometimes it is impossible to gather evidence before making a generalization. Instead, the generalization must be made first and then tested.

To illustrate: Art Loomis is what is commonly known as a "rockhound," an amateur geologist. People often give him interesting rocks they have picked up in their travels. Recently he received a specimen from a man who had visited the Monterey coast in California. The man said that his specimen was jade.

Art knew that jade is often found on the coast near Monterey. He also knew (from previous induction) that the rock looked something like jade. Therefore, he could say: "For the sake of argument, I'll assume that this rock is jade. If it is, there are certain tests, of hardness, structure, and so on, that the rock should meet." Art went through these tests one by one and, sure enough, the rock passed them all. He then felt justified in saying: "The hypothesis is confirmed. This rock is jade."

Now, it is possible that one of the tests might not have worked. In that case, Art would have abandoned his original hypothesis and set up a new, equally plausible one to be tested. Eventually he would have discovered the true nature of the rock.

Notice that in setting up a hypothesis, you must already have some knowledge of the subject. Art knew enough about jade to realize that he wasn't working entirely in the dark. If he had said, "For the sake of argument, I'll assume that this rock is coral," he would have been working from complete ignorance. The rock had none of the characteristics of coral, and Art knew it. A hypothesis of coral would have been the wildest kind of guessing—not really a hypothesis at all, but a foolish attempt to ouija-board prophecy.

The setting up and testing of hypotheses is so much a part of everyday life that you do it unconsciously—but it is a very valuable technique of logic. It is worth applying consciously to a wide variety of business and professional problems.

TECHNIQUES OF DEDUCTIVE REASONING ══════

Inductive reasoning always precedes deductive reasoning. Almost every generalization that people believe—"grass is usually green," "the highway death toll is appalling"—was reached by a process of induction. Only after such a generalization has been reached can deductive reasoning proceed.

What is deductive reasoning? Well, for one thing, it is the opposite of inductive reasoning. Rather than gathering bits and pieces of information and then reaching a conclusion, you start at the other end. You begin with a generalization that you are willing to accept as true. Then you apply this generalization to specific cases. You work from the general to the specific instead of from the specific to the general. The classic example:

Major Premise.   All men are mortal.
Minor Premise.   Socrates is a man.
Conclusion.   Therefore, Socrates is mortal.

The form in which these statements appear is called a *syllogism*. Deductive reasoning is *syllogistic* reasoning, a very useful device if you work from valid premises, follow the syllogistic form exactly, and don't get bogged down in a mass of academic jargon.

The most important point to remember about deductive reasoning is that *the major premise is almost never stated directly.* Once you recognize that fact, you will see how common deductive reasoning is. Remember: The syllogistic form is seldom used in its entirety, except by befuddled youngsters in formal logic courses. Instead, only the conclusion is stated; the premises are implied.

When your friend makes a simple statement like "Harry has been fired," she may be reasoning deductively. Suppose your friend has seen Harry remove a pink slip from his pay envelope. From this fact, she has reached a conclusion. Thus:

Major Premise.   A pink slip in a pay envelope is always a notice of dismissal.
Minor Premise.   A pink slip was in Harry's pay envelope.
Conclusion.   Therefore, Harry has been dismissed.

An academic logician might object to the wording of the syllogism (mainly because academic logicians seem more concerned with verbal niceties than with meaning), but nothing is wrong with the reasoning involved.

The conclusion could be wrong, of course. Let's say Harry comes over to your friend and shows her the slip. It says: "This check reflects your recent salary increase. If you have any questions concerning it, please contact Miss Frankel in Personnel." The major premise was wrong.

Or it could be that your friend observed inaccurately. The slip in Harry's envelope was orange, not pink—a notice concerning social security payments, not dismissal. The minor premise was wrong.

But if the major premises were both right, the conclusion was inevitably right. That is the great strength of the syllogism. If you can work from absolutely certain premises, you cannot go wrong. The trouble is that many premises, principally abstract major premises, are *not* absolutely certain. Thus, when Sherlock Holmes says to John Hector McFarland, "I assure you that beyond the obvious facts that you are a bachelor, a solicitor, a Freemason, and an asthmatic, I know nothing whatever about you," he is simply whistling in the wind. He bases his conclusion of bachelorhood on one fact: McFarland is dressed untidily. Holmes's major premise is that all men who dress untidily are bachelors. And that major premise is as wild as a wounded boar.

When reasoning deductively, you should observe the following rules:

- Know the major premise that you are reasoning from. If necessary, state your major premise.

- Make sure that your major premise is sound. Reason inductively to determine the soundness of a major premise.

- Check the validity of your reasoning. One example will suffice: "All doctors are college graduates. O'Rourke is not a college graduate. Therefore, O'Rourke is a truck driver." Eh?

FIVE LOGICAL FALLACIES ================================

O'Rourke, it turns out, is a millionaire oil man. Well, it's easy to laugh and say, "Sure, but I don't make mistakes like that." Unfortunately, though, you probably do. I do, my colleagues do, and I have the impression that nearly everyone else does once in a while. In fact, logical fallacies are so common in the newspapers, on television, and in ordinary conversation that the only defense against them is to learn as much as you can about them—what they are, why they occur, and how to combat them.

There are five logical fallacies which are epidemic. Here they are

1. Inadequate sampling

A salesperson once confessed to his sales manager that he couldn't sell the company's product, a name-brand typewriter. Other salespeople were selling it, said the manager. True, but this one wasn't. Nobody seemed to need new typewriters. OK, said the manager. Start at the top of the office building you're in right now. Just go up to everyone you see and ask, "You don't need a new typewriter, do you?"—the worst possible sales technique. Doubtfully, the salesperson started off. Within an hour, a purchasing agent responded to his odd question: "Yes, our company needs about twenty new typewriters; but good grief, you can't sell typewriters with your approach." "You're telling me," said the salesperson and they sat down to discuss sales techniques—and typewriters. The salesperson sold twenty typewriters, went right on through the building with the same negative approach,and sold fifty more. So, you see, at least seventy new typewriters *were* needed, and right in the salesperson's own building. Previously, the man's sampling had been inadequate.

One famous case of inadequate sampling is the 1936 *Literary Digest* poll fiasco. The magazine asked hundreds of thousands of people how they would vote in the upcoming Presidential election. Alf Landon won the poll hands down. Franklin D. Roosevelt then carried 46 of the 48 states in the election. Why was the poll so far off? The answer is now well known. For its sampling the

Digest used the telephone exclusively. But a telephone in those depression days was a luxury, possessed mostly by the "haves" rather than by the "have-nots." The "haves" wanted Landon, but there were a lot more "have-nots." "The have-nots" won, and after the election few people wanted the *Literary Digest.* The sampling of the *Digest* had been extensive but not representative. As surely as in the case of the typewriter salesperson, the sampling had been inadequate.

2. *Post hoc, ergo propter hoc*

This Latin expression means "after this, therefore because of this." The flowering of Elizabethan literature came after the defeat of the Spanish Armada. Therefore, the defeat *caused* the flowering of Elizabethan literature. Did it? Garrett Mattingly, author of the best-known book on the defeat of the Spanish Armada, says cautiously that no one knows. But probably, he implies, it didn't; there is no good reason to see a connection between the two events. *Post hoc, ergo propter hoc.*

Superstitions are based almost wholly on this very common *post hoc* fallacy. Disaster will follow walking under a ladder, seeing a black cat, staying on the thirteenth floor of a hotel. Even if disaster occasionally *does* follow such an event, there is no rational reason to suppose that the first incident *caused* the second. A student of mine once said, "I've noticed that whenever I fail a test, I've had a bottle of Coke just before taking it." Well, all right. He can blame his failure on anything he wishes, but he would be more in the spirit of things at the Mad Hatter's tea party than in a college classroom.

3. *False analogy*

William H. Whyte, Jr., tells the fascinating story of the corporation that foolishly likened its employees to a football team. "Isn't a company just like a great big team?" they asked. "Isn't a company out to win sales in the same way that a team is out to win victories?" Their answers were yes, and posthaste they started out to recruit the invincible team. Soon the office was bouncing with bright, personable young men and women. The eager, new team was just about ready to go, ready to charge across the fifty-yard line. Alas! The competing companies, plodding along with the same tired old veterans, had already crossed the goal line with a new product. The football analogy hadn't quite worked.

A company, concludes Whyte, is *not* just like a football team. Similarly, a governmental budget is *not* just like a personal budget. A packaged pain reliever is *not* just like a doctor's prescription. A computer is *not* just like a human brain.

Beware of all such false analogies. They are as pernicious as they are appealing. Analogies can be useful in describing certain complex objects or ideas, but they can also be deadly booby traps unless they are used with extreme caution.

4. Non sequitur

A non sequitur is a conclusion that does not follow logically from the premises. For instance, people have often said to me, "Oh, of course you're a Republican; you're from upstate New York." The fact is, however, that there are a lot of people in upstate New York who are registered Democrats. To assume as a major premise that all upstaters are Republicans is palpably silly. The conclusion from such an assumption is a non sequitur.

5. Undefined abstractions

Perhaps the most common logical fallacy is this one, based on semantics. Remember, words do not mean the same thing to everyone. What is a "flaming liberal" to me may be an "arch conservative" to you. Even when you use the classic syllogism, "All men are mortal," you cannot be completely sure that you will be understood. "Men" *could* mean males only, though clearly the thought should be intended for men *and* women. But how about "mortal"? Does "mortal" mean merely that all men die; and if so, does it mean that they die physically, or spiritually, or both? Probably "physically," but there is no need to belabor the point. Words can confuse issues as well as clarify them. The uses and abuses of words have already been discussed many times in this book. The one point that is vital to power thinking is this: Unless you can make your listener or reader agree on the meanings of words, there can be no worthwhile communication, and no valid logic.

HOWS AND WHYS OF THE SCIENTIFIC METHOD

A discussion of logic would not be complete without a brief mention of the scientific method. The scientific method, properly used, is a valuable tool for combining inductive and deductive reasoning; moreover, its uses are not limited to the rarefied atmosphere of science. Assuming that scientists have found exceptionally accurate ways to work out problems, these methods ought to be applicable to the workaday world—and they are!

Here are the steps involved in using the scientific method:

1. A problem is recognized and an objective is set up.
2. All of the relevant available information is collected.
3. A working hypothesis is formulated.
4. Deductions are drawn from the hypothesis.
5. The deductions are tested by actual trial.
6. Depending on the outcome, the working hypothesis is accepted, modified, or discarded.

This may sound like a pretty cold, analytical approach to nonscientific problems. It is true that if the rigid formula presented here truly represented the working scientist's thought processes—or anyone else's—it would bear out the philosophers' conception of a wholly rational human. Most scientists would probably agree, however, with Dr. C. G. Suits of General Electric when he said of that fictitious character: "I've yet to meet him. Candidly, I doubt that he exists; and if he did exist, I fear that he would never make a startling discovery or invention."

No, the scientific method is not a set of hard and fast rules by which it is possible to solve the riddles of the universe. Neither is it nothing more than everyday common sense. It is a sound, sensible method for solving at least some of the problems that arise on the job. When the six-step formula is carefully and thoughtfully followed, it can yield results that no amount of random thought could ever yield.

You can easily see which parts of the scientific method are inductive (steps 1, 2, and 3) and which parts are deductive (steps 4, 5, and 6). You can also see, I'm sure, that by combining both of these power-thinking devices into a single plan of attack you have at your fingertips a dynamic, workable approach to problems that demand extensive reasoning.

As Dr. Suits points out, you will not go through this formula every time you are faced with a situation calling for the use of logic. But knowing about the scientific method and using it when it is appropriate to major problems will give you a real key to occupational success.

LOGIC IN ACTION

For a demonstration of logic in action, it is worth reading Edgar Allan Poe's "The Mystery of Marie Rogêt." In this story, Poe, working solely from newspaper accounts of a crime, shows how he actually solved a murder that had baffled police for weeks. This story is not the ordinary Sherlock Holmes nonsense. The plot is slightly fictionalized by Poe, but the murder and its solution are, or were, verv real. The logic of Poe (or "Dupin," as he calls the hero) is sound throughout. In fact, "The Mystery of Marie Rogêt" is a major masterpiece of inductive and deductive reasoning in action.

A brief excerpt from the story may show you what I mean. The newspapers had maintained that the murder of a young woman was the work of a gang of ruffians. Poe, as Dupin, does not believe it. Left behind at the scene of the crime—a secluded, wooded area—had been a petticoat, a scarf, a parasol, gloves, and a handkerchief bearing the name "Marie Rogêt." Poe reasons that an individual, not a gang, would have left this evidence behind:

> If this was an accident [the clothes being left behind] it was not the accident of a gang. We can imagine it only as the accident of an individual. Let us see. An individual has committed the murder. He is alone with the ghost of the departed. He is appalled with what lies motionless before him. The fury of his passion is over, and there is abundant room in his heart for the natural awe of the deed. He trembles and is bewildered. Yet there is a necessity for disposing of the corpse. He bears it to the river, and leaves behind him the

other evidence of his guilt; for it is difficult, if not impossible, to carry all the burthen at once, and it will be easy to return for what is left. But in his toilsome journey to the river his fears redouble within him. The sounds of life encompass his path. A dozen times he hears or fancies he hears the step of an observer. Even the very lights from the city bewilder him. Yet, in time, and by long and frequent pauses of deep agony, he reaches the river's brink and disposes of his ghastly charge. But *now* what treasure does the world hold—what threat of vengeance could it hold out—which would have the power to urge the return of that lonely murderer over that toilsome and perilous path to the thicket and its blood-chilling recollections? He returns *not*, let the consequences be what they may. He *could* not return if he would. His sole thought is immediate escape. He turns his back forever upon those dreadful shrubberies, and flees as from the wrath to come.

But how with a gang? Their number would have inspired them with confidence; if, indeed, confidence is ever wanting in the breast of the arrant blackguard; and of arrant blackguards alone are the supposed gangs ever constituted. Their number, I say, would have prevented the bewildering and unreasoning terror which I have imagined to paralyze the single man. Could we suppose an oversight in one, or two, or three, this oversight would have been remedied by the fourth. They would have left nothing behind them; for their number would have enabled them to carry all at once. There would have been no need of return.

And Poe was right; the newspapers were wrong. For a convincing demonstration of the power of logical thought, by all means read "The Mystery of Marie Rogêt." You will discover in it many techniques that you can apply to problems much less tragic than the murder of a beautiful young woman.

TEN TIPS FOR LOGICAL THINKING

1. Wherever possible, gather evidence before reaching a conclusion.
2. Be careful of generalizations containing the words *all*, *always*, and *never*. There are very few rules which do not have exceptions.

3. Examine statistics with an eagle eye. Statistics can lie, and many statistics are nothing more than special pleading.

4. Beware of the words *average* and *typical*. These are often words of prejudice, not reason.

5. Learn how to make sensible hypotheses. Don't just guess at answers to problems; set up a method for testing them.

6. In reasoning deductively, make sure you know what your major premise is. Determine whether this major premise is really true.

7. Always check your reasoning to make sure it is valid. Avoid inadequate sampling, *post hoc, ergo propter hoc* fallacies, false analogy, and non sequiturs.

8. Remember that logic involves the meanings of words. Even after something has been logically proved to your satisfaction, it will not necessarily be accepted by everyone.

9. Consider using the scientific method to solve major problems, especially long-term, on-the-job problems.

10. Read and listen carefully and critically. Recognize logical fallacies in the arguments of others. Try to eliminate logical fallacies from your own arguments.

Chapter 11

Mental Dynamics of Creating Ideas

- Your Ability to Create Ideas
- Sparking Ideas
- Effort, Plus
- First Create, Then Judge
- Prod Your Curiosity
- But I'm No Genius
- Your Own Ivory Tower
- Set a Goal for Ideation
- Make Yourself Create
- Trust Your Own Ability
- One Idea Leads to Another
- Have Lots of Alternatives
- Discovery Is the Essence
- Ten Tips for Ideation

In the case of gemstones, collectors' coins, and old prints, the measure of value is rarity. What is rare is desirable. According to this criterion, a person's creativity—his or her power to generate ideas—should be a priceless personal asset. Few people will deny that it is. Corporations would rather pay $75,000 a year to a true "idea person" than $25,000 a year to a person who lacks ideas. Business people, education leaders, and government officials are constantly demanding men and women with imaginative new ideas. The person who can deliver on that demand is sure to have a brilliant future.

Ideation, the creation of new ideas, is the vital spark of personal and corporate progress. "This is probably a nutty idea" is one of the least nutty sentences you can utter. Without so-called nutty ideas, business would come to a standstill. Humankind would be frozen to the past, to the tried and true, to the horse and buggy. Without "nutty" ideas, your own progress may be severely limited. To succeed, you must be able to unleash your mind and make it roam into new and unexplored regions. You *can* do it. There are thousands of ideas waiting to be dreamed up. There are thousands of questions waiting to be answered.

One key word is involved in most questions that lead to true creative thought. It is the tiny word, *why? Why* can't monorails replace commuter buses? *Why* can't all newspapers be of tabloid size? *Why* isn't there a spread sheet program that's easier to learn? *Why* isn't there a clock radio/CD player?

Some of these questions remain to be answered, while to some of them the answers are seemingly known; but all such questions have one thing in common: They force you to open your mind to ideas, not necessarily to create a new product or method, but at least to *think* about ideation.

Admitting the value of imaginative new ideas, you may still ask, "Can creativity be developed?" The answer is that it can. Although only an Einstein could work out the theory of relativity, it did not take a genius to suggest drip coffeemakers or compact cars. In fact, most of the new ideas that you come across every day were thought up by ordinary people whose imaginations were working overtime. These people kept asking themselves "Why?", and they came up with the answers. You can do the same thing.

YOUR ABILITY TO CREATE IDEAS

What, exactly, is creative ability? An obvious answer is that it is the ability to create. But to create what, and under what circumstances, and for whom? There is a real problem in semantics here. Everyone knows that Rembrandt, Shakespeare, Edison, and Ford were creative geniuses. Most people would consider advertising copywriters, popular song composers, and choreographers to be in creative lines of work. There are even those who regard good cooks and outstanding auto mechanics as having creative ability. But with all due respect to Mrs. Filstrup down the road, there is a whale of a difference between creating *Hamlet* and creating ham omelets.

Whole books have been written on creativity without the authors' ever having once defined their key word. And no wonder—it's a hard word to pin down. Still, unless an attempt is made, the whole discussion is likely to bog down. So here we go: "Creativity is the human trait that leads to the mental creation of unique and workable new ideas, products, or methods." It must be added that there are *degrees* of creativity. Creativity ranges from the highest of imaginative fancy (James Joyce's *Ulysses*) to an idea for the most utilitarian object (a better mousetrap). But the' creation is basically *mental*. There may be a product at the end of the process, but it's the *idea* that represents creativity.

Let's look at an example of creativity. John McAdam, a nineteenth-century Scottish engineer, served as a road trustee in Ayrshire, Scotland. He observed that the roads in his district were in very poor condition. After pondering the question of how to effect reforms, he hit upon the idea of using crushed stone as a paving material. Today, whether you drive on a "macadam" road or a concrete road, you own a debt of gratitude to this man for whom the old way of road building wasn't good enough. McAdam was creative. He had an idea that has spread throughout the civilized world.

Wherever you look—at home, in shopping centers, or on the highway—you see the results of creative effort. The process of creation is a never-ending one, yet few people contribute as much as they can to it. Most of us are willing to go on watching and using the results of creative effort, without ever buckling down to genuine creative work of our own. The time to change that situation is *now*.

SPARKING IDEAS

Nearly every large corporation spends money on research and development. The men and women who do this research receive their salaries for being creative. Day after day they experiment with new processes and new products. Not all of them will be as successful as Dr. Charles Stine and Dr. Wallace Carothers, the men who first synthesized Du Pont nylon; but all of them are working toward creative goals.

The important word is "working." For creativity does require effort; flashes of inspiration are rare. The person who sparks new ideas is usually a tireless worker. He or she has to be, for creative thinking is exhausting work, and the rewards are often few and far between.

Thomas A. Edison is the classic case of an inventive genius. Because Edison had so many remarkable ideas, there is a common misconception that new ideas came effortlessly to him, much as Coleridge "saw" the poem "Kubla Khan" in an opium dream. Nonsense! Edison worked very hard to be creative. He had no illusions about ideas just popping into his head. He knew that creativity requires effort, and he spent his life putting forth that effort in full measure.

EFFORT, PLUS . . .

But effort alone is not enough. It may be good fun to brush in the right colors on a paint-by-the-numbers canvas, but it is hardly creative. Nor is it creative, though it may be relaxing, to refinish furniture in a basement workshop. Creativity is essentially mental, not physical. The person who *originated the idea* of painting by numbers was creative, and so was the person who sparked the idea behind better varnish removers. Creativity requires mental effort *and* imagination.

We all know people who put in a sixty-hour work week, never arrive late, never leave early, and never get anywhere. Their problem is not physical laziness; it is mental torpor. The people fail to understand the value of just one good, original idea. It is always a little sad to see them bypassed by eager new workers who put high priority on ideas as well as on technical details.

A vivid imagination, a willingness to take mental leaps into the unknown, an inquiring frame of mind—these must be added to solid effort if creativity is to take hold.

FIRST CREATE, THEN JUDGE

All too frequently we apply hasty judgments to new ideas—our own as well as others. "If the idea were any good, someone else would have thought of it." "We've tried it before, Sue." "It's too wild a scheme for the boss to buy." These are negative attitudes that will stop ideation cold.

Ideation demands a certain amount of "nutty" day dreaming. To come up with new products, methods, and ideas, you must turn your mind loose. You must get it out of the well-worn grooves. You must "think big" and you must "think different." A soaring imagination cannot be chained to negative logic.

Once you do have a truly original idea, though, you should apply sound judgment to it. There is no point in rushing to the boss with a half-thought-out idea. If your idea really is good, you can perhaps make it a lot better by thinking judicially about it. At that point, you can look for pitfalls and try to find ways around them. But judgment should come only after imaginative effort, not before it.

Imagine, create, and then judge—that's the proper order.

PROD YOUR CURIOSITY

Creative people are curious people. They want to know how things work, or why they don't work. They are interested in everything that goes on around them. They are constantly learning and testing new ideas. From their vast storehouse of experiences, they are able to generate new ideas of their own. Ben Franklin and Thomas Jefferson were such men. Their range of interests covered almost all human knowledge.

Noncreative people, on the other hand, are seldom curious about anything. They pass through life with blinders on. Even when they look closely at something, they do not really see it. What they experience they do not make a part of their usable knowledge. They are seldom excited about the world around them. Niagara Falls: "It looks just like in the movies." Men and women in space: "A big waste of money. There's nothing out there." Urban renewal: "This city will always be a dump."

I received a postcard not long ago from a student who was traveling in Europe. The card was postmarked Mannheim, and the student had written: "I'm seeing the Rhine for the first time. It's great. Lots of castles. Jugs and jugs of fabulous Rhine wine and German beer." And I thought of how Oliver Wendell Holmes had described the same experience:

> I saw the green banks of the castle-crowned Rhine,
> Where the grapes drink the moonlight and change it to wine.

In assessing the difference between these two statements, I thought of the student's all-too-common "gut by" attitude. Then I thought of Holmes's bubbling drive, his boundless curiosity. The elder Henry James had said to him, "Holmes, you are intellectually the most alive man I ever knew." And the old doctor had replied, "I am, I am! From the crown of my head to the sole of my foot, I'm alive!"

Holmes was also highly creative. In this respect he was not unique among innovators. It is safe to say that intellectual aliveness and burning curiosity are traits possessed by every creative thinker.

BUT I'M NO GENIUS

Creativity is not tied to intelligence, education, age, or sex. According to Dr. C. G. Suits of General Electric, "*Everyone has hunches. No one is wholly without some spark. And that spark,* however small, is capable of being blown on until it burns more brightly."

The Wildroot Company was founded by two barbers who used to work in Buffalo's Iroquois Hotel. The company achieved leadership in its field under a man who had driven a junk wagon in his early years. All three of these men were highly creative, despite their apparently "noncreative" backgrounds.

The number of people who have demonstrated creativity without the benefit of a high school or college education is legion. During the Second World War, many of the most imaginative ideas came from people who would not ordinarily be thought of as creative.

Sergeant Culin was one such person. Soon after the invasion of Normandy, the Allied armies ran into a formidable obstacle: hedgerows in the bocage country of France. These rows were high, dense hedges surrounding small plots of ground. Generally they grew out of a bank of earth three or four feet high. When Allied tanks tried to cross the hedgerows, which were often fortified, their unarmored bellies offered a perfect target. Also, their own guns were useless in that position. None of the brass could figure out a solution to this problem. Enter Sergeant Culin. He suggested putting two blades of steel on the front of each tank. The plan worked, and the tanks equipped with blades advanced on an even keel, cutting through both earth and hedges, picking up camouflage on the way.

So don't be discouraged. You may prove just as creative as a Ph.D. physicist working in pure research. Give your creativity a fair try!

YOUR OWN IVORY TOWER

Where can you do your creative thinking? Well, you can do creative thinking almost anywhere. One of the most imaginative people I know says that he does his best work on the subway during rush hours: "I close my eyes, forget the bustle around me, and try to joggle my mind. I spend more than an hour a day on the subway, and I usually manage to put this time to good creative use."

The subway may seem like an odd place for creative thought. There are certainly more common places. Some people find that they think best in the shower, others in bed, still others on long, solitary walks. I met a person once who claimed that his best creative effort came after a glass of wine before dinner.

"I have no place at home where I can think." Excuses like that are rationalizations more often than not. With a little ingenuity, you can find the proper time and place to create. Where you work best may be quite different from any of the places mentioned, but that's natural. Your own "ivory tower," just like your own ideas, will be uniquely personal.

SET A GOAL FOR IDEATION

Most creative ideas do not spring up without prior thought. "Get your mind whirling," said psychologist William James, "and see what happens."

Generally speaking, you have to think quite a while about a question before you arrive at a creative answer. Edison had to, and so did Steinmetz, Ford, and Kettering. Each of these men worked toward specific goals. The Wright brothers didn't say to themselves, "There must be better methods of transportation around." Or perhaps they did—at first. But when they really got down to work, they knew *precisely* what they were after.

You must be specific about your goals. If a person wants to write a book, she has to decide what kind of book, of what length, and for what market. An editor I know says that she is amazed by the number of coaches who want to write how-to-do-it books on "football." Now, one doesn't just write a book on football these days. She writes on some specific aspect of it. Try to picture Herman Melville telling his publisher, "Well, I don't know. I'm thinking about writing a book on whales."

To think creatively, you should have a goal clearly in mind. On the job it may be "How can we improve the sales of Zip-Dee-Doo candy bars in Cleveland?" Or "How can we produce a better electric clock for cars?" Or "How can we cut losses on our overstock of stuffed owls?"

Notice that a "why" question probably preceded each of these "how" questions: "*Why* are Zip-Dee-Doo sales dropping in Cleveland?" "*Why* are the present automobile clocks unsatisfactory?" "*Why* are all those stuffed owls still sitting on the showroom floor?" In other words, the "how" question itself is somewhat creative. For while the "why" question is general, the "how" question is specific. And that's the first giant step in working out a solution.

In going from general to specific questions, you will occasionally strike the right answer immediately. The person who started with the question "Why can't a phonograph be put into the same cabinet with a radio?" didn't have to ask very many "how's." The answer was inherent in the question. But usually you must plan on working down, quite consciously, from general questions to specific questions, from specific questions to specific answers.

MAKE YOURSELF CREATE

Since flashes of inspiration are rare, it stands to reason that you must sometimes *make* yourself create. Setting a deadline for creativity may sound like utter nonsense. But it isn't. Consider the people who write advertising copy. They can't simply wait for lightning to strike. They have deadlines to meet. They must try to make lightning strike.

And how about newspaper reporters? They can't wait until next week or next month to write about today's news. Yet sometimes they write creatively. So do headline and caption writers. I can still remember a photo caption I saw years ago in the *Elmira Advertiser*. It appeared on the day that Hitler committed suicide. Over a picture of the Führer, the caption read, "Report Nazi Tyrant at End of Trail." The Old West expression "end of trail" creates a rather odd image. Nevertheless, anyone who could write, almost on a moment's notice, a caption that I would remember for four decades certainly had some sort of creative spark.

Courtroom lawyers, too, have to be creatively resourceful. Their deadlines are often measured in seconds. A high point in such instant creativity was reached many years ago by Rufus Choate. Choate was trying a case in the Westchester area north of the Bronx. The opposing lawyer was a local man who wished to contrast his personality with that of Choate, a suave New Yorker. To the jury the local lawyer said earnestly, "I hope you won't be influenced by my opponent's Chesterfieldian urbanity." The jury looked impressed. Immediately Choate arose and said to the jury, with perfect composure, "And by the same token, I hope you won't be influenced by my opponent's Westchesterfieldian suburbanity." It brought down the house.

Yes, creativity can be harnessed to a deadline, occasionally even to a split-second deadline, as in the case of Choate. Set yourself a deadline and see.

TRUST YOUR OWN ABILITY

Good ideas are so valuable that none should ever be lost in the shuffle. Unfortunately, they sometimes are, because of people's natural timidity about putting forth their own thoughts. "Oh, my ideas can't be any good," you think. And consequently they aren't. Nobody ever hears of them. Don't let it happen, for your ideas are likely to be as good as the next person's.

Charlie Rockwell tells about a contest he almost entered. A lumber company was offering a $1000 prize for the best phrase describing cedar. Charlie wrote on a piece of paper. "The Wood Eternal." No, he thought—too corny. He put it aside. Months later he saw a magazine advertisement for cedar. Across the top of the page, in large letters, it said, "Cedar: The Wood Eternal." Someone got that $1000, but it wasn't Charlie Rockwell. He never bothered to suggest his idea.

Nobody knows how many good ideas have been irretrievably lost, but the number must run into the millions. And it's so unnecessary. The majority of people will welcome a bright new idea, particularly if it's modestly presented. Don't say or imply, "Damn it, here's my plan. Buy it or else." Instead, try the tactful approach: "Maybe you've already thought of this, but . . ."

So break out those "crazy" ideas. Talk them up. They just may work!

ONE IDEA LEADS TO ANOTHER

The most useful spur to your creativity is undoubtedly the principle of association. You may see a relationship between one thing and another, between one idea and another—a relationship that has never been seen before. You make use of this relationship to create a new product, method, or plan. The principle of association as a key to creativity has been recognized for a long time. The ancient Greeks named three laws of association: (1) contiguity, (2) similarity, and (3) contrast.

Contiguity means simply "adjoining" or "in a continuous mass or series." Most of the major parts of the automobile, for example, were developed and improved according to the law of contiguity. Take fenders. The first fenders, like those on the 1903 Oldsmobile, were nothing but sheets of steel placed so as to fend off flying mud. Later, fenders were curved over the front wheels and were swept back slightly. Thus, on the 1912 Maxwell the fenders were functional but also decorative. In the 1920s and 1930s, fenders were swept farther and farther back on the body. By the 1950s, most cars had fenders that were wholly a part of the body. Today, fenders have nearly disappeared.

Each new fender design was a creative idea, but each one was also part of a developmental pattern. Manufacturers did not take one huge leap from the design of the 1903 Oldsmobile to that of the 1990 Cadillac. Rather, they took many small steps along the way. Through the creative efforts of designers, automobile bodies will no doubt continue to evolve according to this contiguous pattern.

In planning your own creative efforts, you should keep in mind the law of contiguity. Ask yourself, "How can this product, method, or idea be developed further?" "How can it be improved?"

The law of similarity also leads to creative new ideas. At the time I was growing up, it was axiomatic that young children had tricycles and older children had bicycles. That arrangement seemed logical and unalterable. Tricycles were stable and would not tip over, while bicycles were unstable and required a mature sense of balance. But then some creative person took a close, clear look at similarities. So now we have bicycles with training wheels. These removable wheels prevent bicycles from tipping over and consequently make them as safe as tricycles.

When working creatively, you should ask yourself these questions: "In what way is *this* product, method, or idea similar to *that* one?" How can the similarities be transferred from one to the other?"

Contrast is perhaps less useful than contiguity or similarity, yet it does have its functions. It is especially worthwhile in advertising. When a manufacturer of fibers wanted to demonstrate the strengths of these fibers in rugs, a creative person asked herself, "Where would a rug seem *least* practical because of the hard wear it would get?" Her answer: "The locker room of a major league baseball team." To most people it would appear impossible that any rug could stand up to the incessant pounding of baseball spikes. The company installed wall-to-wall carpeting in the locker room of the New York Yankees and used this carpeting as the basis of full-page, four-color magazine advertisements.

The creative person will ask herself, "How can we turn this present idea inside-out, upside-down?" "How can we do exactly the opposite of what is now being done or what now seems "the only sensible way'?"

HAVE LOTS OF ALTERNATIVES

When you look around your kitchen, you may assume that the brand names of the appliances and products found there just popped into someone's head and were forthwith applied to the product. In some cases, that's true. But today it is much more likely that a brand name or model name was chosen from hundreds or even thousands of reasonably good alternatives.

If many alternatives are desirable in choosing such names, so too are many choices worthwhile in other creative efforts. "But," you say, "it's hard enough to think up one creative idea. Now I have to dream up a hundred!" Not quite. For one thing, a basic idea may itself suggest many alternatives. You are not expected, like Edison, to invent a number of totally different things. You are merely advised to think about a number of variations on a single theme.

Another point about alternatives: When you are in an exceptionally creative mood, you may come up with half a dozen different ideas. It would be foolish not to jot them all down for further consideration. In fact, the idea that seemed the worst at the time may, upon careful reflection, prove to be the best. The more alternatives you have, the better are your chances for hitting upon the one great idea that will spread around the world.

DISCOVERY IS THE ESSENCE

Critics of American life often lament that our creative powers as a nation have declined in recent years. They point out that creativity is seldom taught, seldom even encouraged, in the public schools, and that students concentrate instead on learning Gradgrind's "facts, facts, facts." Yankee ingenuity, they say, is consequently declining.

The power thinker must teach himself to be imaginative, inquisitive, and adaptable. The deadly enemy of creativity is conformity, or the acceptance of things as they are. To be genuinely creative, a power thinker must force himself to think in new dimensions, to try promising new schemes, to seek imaginative solutions for old problems.

It can be done, and it may change your life.

TEN TIPS FOR IDEATION

1. Remember that ideation can be developed. It is definitely possible to learn the techniques of creating unique and workable new ideas, products, and methods.

2. Put forth the effort necessary to be creative. New ideas do not just fly in through an open window. You must go out and look for them.

3. Cultivate a vivid imagination, an inquiring mind, and a willingness to take mental leaps from the ordinary to the extraordinary.

4. Create before you judge what your creative efforts will yield. Don't adopt a negative attitude toward new ideas, either other people's or your own.

5. Prod your curiosity. When you look, make sure you see. When you listen, make sure you hear. Develop ever-broader interests and seek ever broader experiences.

6. Don't downgrade your own creativity. Creative ability is not confined to gilt-edge, hand-tooled products of prestige colleges and universities.

7. Find the proper time and place for doing your best creative thinking. Avoid rationalizing that you can't discover any such time or place.

8. When ideas occur to you, jot them down on paper. Don't take a chance on losing your best thoughts.

9. Set a specific goal for your creative efforts. Work down from general to specific problems and questions.

10. Learn the principles of association, the laws of contiguity, similarity, and contrast. Whenever possible, have a number of alternatives for each basic idea.

Chapter 12

Fourteen Steps to Personal Power

LEADERSHIP, THE ESSENCE OF PERSONAL POWER, is not easy to define. Leaders are as varied as humanity itself. Some leaders are outgoing and aggressive; others are shy and retiring. Some achieve their leadership through technical competence. Others achieve it through force of personality, despite a lack of technical know-how. A leader may be brusque or genial, calm or restless, clever or phlegmatic, tall or short, young or old, male or female.

These differences exist partly because jobs vary. A director of chemical research is perhaps less personable than a sales manager in a toy company; nevertheless, she may be every bit as effective. The people she leads are different, the job is different, the goals are different. Leadership cannot be separated from the specific job. The world's best sales manager for toys would probably fail as a director of chemical research. Likewise, a chemical research director would no doubt flounder in trying to whip up enthusiasm for dolls.

Yet the research director and the sales manager are both leaders. They both direct the activities of other people. If they are good leaders, they are respected for their abilities and well compensated for their work.

The first question about leadership, then, is this: Leadership *for what?* The young Douglas MacArthur was a brilliant battlefield leader. Franklin D. Roosevelt was a superb political leader. The presidents of General Motors and IBM are outstanding business leaders. These people are all quite different from one another. A person attains leadership in a certain field, at a particular time. His traits are the ones required then and there, but not ones that can be unerringly laid out on a chart and reliably predicted by an aptitude test.

The second question is this: *Are there any traits that seem to characterize good leaders regardless of their specific jobs?* The answer is yes. Most people who have studied the dynamics of leadership have ended their discussion with a list of traits that do seem to characterize many outstanding leaders. These traits are not universal among leaders, of course, nor are they present in all leaders to the same degree. A few leaders are so strong in some respects that their weaknesses in other respects can be over-looked. However, if you plan to develop your own leadership potential to the fullest, you will want to examine carefully the qualities that are often found in leaders in every field.

THE MARKS OF LEADERSHIP

Here are the qualities that usually characterize leaders. Although there is no such thing as a "perfect" leader, the person who possesses these qualities undoubtedly has great potential.

1. The leader has an overpowering urge for action. He wants to get ahead. He sets goals for himself and spares no efforts to achieve them.

2. The leader has a positive self-image. She sees herself far more realistically than most people are able to see themselves. She has an excellent idea of how others see her.

3. The leader has self-confidence. He trusts his own ability and does not lose his head in a crisis.

4. The leader is decisive. She dares to make decisions and stick to them. She seizes opportunities that others might miss.

5. The leader makes sound judgments. He knows that decisiveness coupled with poor judgment is disastrous. When he decides, therefore, he usually decides correctly.

6. The leader gets along well with people. A leader, by definition, must have followers. The leader respects her followers, gives them a feeling of accomplishment, and recognizes their potential for growth.

7. The leader has empathy. Not only does he get along with people on a "Good morning, Joe" basis, he also is able to put himself into their shoes—indeed, into their minds. He has insight into the motivation of others.

8. The leader knows how to plan and organize. She does not, like the Leacock character, jump on her horse and ride madly off in all directions.
9. The leader knows how to delegate authority. He does not get bogged down in details that his subordinates should be able to handle.
10. The leader can take orders as well as given them. Unless she is the top person in her organization, she is a follower as well as a leader. She knows the responsibilities of both.
11. The leader communicates well, both up and down the line. His followers understand what he is saying, and they give him credit for telling the truth.
12. The leader grows into her job, on her job, and into new jobs. She does not become obsolescent as the years pass. She acts her age but "thinks young."
13. The leader blends all his attributes into an integrated whole. He has finesse.
14. The leader has a well-defined set of values. She knows what she wants *from* life, but she also knows what she should contribute *to* life. The leader has a sense of responsibility—personal, professional, local, national, and international.

Most of these qualities can be developed to some extent. Let's look at them more carefully.

MOTIVATION AGAIN

If you have read every chapter in this book, you have come across motivation eleven times. For motivation is the basis of power thinking. It is also the basis of leadership. Unless you have a powerful urge to lead others, to discharge greater responsibilities, and to reach the top, you probably won't. The world is full of people who have every requisite for leadership except motivation.

Stan Randall is such a person. He is a salesperson for an electronics equipment company. He has technical knowledge, self-confidence, personality, and organizational ability. He even "looks like a president." But he never will be, because he doesn't want to be. "I'm satisfied where I am," says Stan. "I enjoy being a successful salesman. I like the variety and challenge of the work." The home office? "It's a rat race back there," says Stan.

Conversely, the salesperson with leadership potential is not satisfied to be forever a salesperson. Although she is likely to be an extremely good one, she has higher goals. She has a gnawing sense of unfulfillment. She knows that she can advance and will advance. She has definite self-chosen goals for personal achievement.

To become a leader, you must want to do so. One expert on executive development has even speculated that you will advance only as far as you want to advance. To illustrate: If you are a salesperson, there are various goals you might have. You might want to be president of the company. Or you might want to stop at vice-president of sales, or at national sales manager, or possibly at district sales manager. You yourself may recognize the actual goal only dimly. But you may already see yourself in one of these jobs—and in no higher one.

The point is, according to this expert, that you are likely to stop at a point no higher than your aspirations. An account executive with presidential potential who says to himself, "I'll be a vice-president of this company someday," will probably be exactly that. He *could* become president, but he *won't*. His progress is initially spurred, but ultimately halted, by his own limited goals.

Now, the obvious reaction to this is, "OK, then, I'll be president. Why set too low a goal?" Not so fast. There are many facets to leadership besides motivation. You may or may not be cut out to be president. Motivation is vital, but, as a power thinker, you must also have a clear realization of your assets *and* your liabilities. You must have a reasonably accurate self-image.

KNOW THYSELF

A timid little man who affects a swagger, munches on a big cigar, and snarls vile oaths is generally regarded as a jerk. He is hardly a unique jerk, though. Holden Caulfield, the young man in Salinger's *Catcher in the Rye*, thought of most adults as "phonies." And, in a way, he had a point. Many people do act out of character, consciously or unconsciously, at least part of the time. They try to appear to be something they are not.

Behaving out of character results from the lack of a realistic self-image. Children often pretend they are cowboys or firefighters or astronauts. That's normal—for children. But when an adult begins to regard himself as Napoleon or Washington or Christ, there is usually a white-coated attendant hovering nearby. The person's self-image has failed completely.

One of the characteristics of a leader is the clear and accurate picture she has of herself. This picture may have been painfully acquired. Everyone has limitations. The leader, unlike the non-leader, knows her faults, tries to correct them where possible, and meanwhile builds on her strong points.

You may be able to acquire a reasonably accurate self-image by taking a long, close, hard look at your self. Look at your appearance, your educational background, your abilities, your liabilities. Ask yourself, "Would I want to be led by me? If not, why not? How can I improve my weaknesses?" Remember, however, that a leader's self-image is almost always positive. She recognizes her weaknesses but she does not feel inhibited or defeated by them.

The responsibility is yours. There is no foolproof checklist for evaluating a self-image. The self-image is too complex and too ingrained to yield to quick and easy analysis. About all that can be said is that if you are able to evaluate yourself well—without serious overrating or underrating—you are a fairly rare person. You have one valuable asset that most leaders have.

TRUST YOURSELF

A leader has self-confidence. He believes in the rightness of the decisions he makes. When he is certain they are right, he will not back down. And he will not lose his head in a crisis. One of the most notable traits of a leader is his refusal to be panicked. Like the Englishman in Churchill's aphorism, as the going gets tougher, so does he.

Self-confidence must be kept within certain bounds, though, if it is not to become self-destructive. We all know people whom others call "supremely self-confident." What they often mean is "foolhardy" or "arrogant." Self-confidence must be tempered by judgment and modesty if it is to be a plus instead of a minus.

Bullies and prigs are self-confident, on the face of things, but they are not leaders.

The kind of self-confidence you need as a leader is the kind that others respect. The confidence you should strive to develop is not the confidence of the conceited, but the confidence of the competent.

LEARN TO MAKE DECISIONS

An executive of the old school is reported to have said to a subordinate, "All you have to do is make decisions and be right 51 percent of the time." That percentage is not quite good enough any more, but the old fellow was on the right track. A leader *must* be able to make decisions, even if she does not have all the information she would like to have.

When President Bush made the decision to invade Panama, he had to act fast on limited information. He had to assume tremendous responsibilities. So did General Eisenhower when he named June 6, 1944, as D-Day. How many Americans, faced with far less serious problems, lean back in their chairs and mutter, "Should I or shouldn't I? Should I or shouldn't I? Should I or shouldn't I?"

It is so easy to state the principle: Learn to make decisions; dare to say "yes" or "no." In practice, however, it seems to be devilishly hard, especially for leaders whose decisions vitally affect the lives of others. Bruce Catton has written that a small voice must have kept whispering to General McClellan, the youthful leader of the Army of the Potomac, "But, general, are you sure?" McClellan never was sure, never made his decisions quickly enough, and was eventually removed from command.

Business decisions are less sanguinary than military decisions, but they are just as important to success. In some companies decision making by junior executives is encouraged; in others it is not. But in nearly every company there is a rather hazy line between the executive responsibilities of, say, a vice-president, and of one of her immediate subordinates. Generally speaking, it is better for the subordinate to take action herself than it is for her to constantly seek the advice and support of her superior. Unless she makes a horrendous mistake, she will be far more highly regarded if she acts on her own whenever the decision is not obviously out of her jurisdiction.

Leaders are expected to make decisions. Indeed, that is the principal reason they are leaders. If it were possible to drift along in her anarchical bliss, with everyone doing whatever struck her fancy, leaders would be unnecessary. But communal living and anarchy don't work. As Harry Truman said, "*Somebody* has to make decisions around here." Yes, and somebody will always have to make the decisions. If you aspire to be a leader at any level, that somebody will be you.

MAKING SOUND JUDGMENTS

A leader must make decisions, but he cannot make them irrationally. If the leader is to be successful, most of his decisions will have to be correct. Thus, decisiveness must be combined with sound judgment.

Teachers often have to make snap decisions that require good judgment. One high school teacher, faced with a serious classroom disciplinary problem involving three students, made a decision of this kind. All three students were over 16 and therefore subject to expulsion. However, they were reasonably good students, likely to graduate if allowed to remain in school. After class, the teacher talked to the students alone and told them that their offense would result in expulsion if reported. The teacher said that she would not report it, but instead would write down an account of the offense, date it, and hold it until the end of the school year. If, during that time, no further offenses of any kind occurred, she would destroy the memorandum. No further offenses occurred, the students graduated, and one of them is now an army captain. The teacher used good judgment.

Business executives must make sound decisions if their companies are to prosper. Every new product that appears on the market represents a decision, one which may involve the expenditure of millions of dollars. An executive who is capable of making such decisions can earn his company (or save his company) a great deal of money. In making decisions of this kind, a business leader must be bold but not rash, cautious but not hidebound. Good judgment is the key.

PERSONALITY OF THE LEADER ═══════════════

A leader almost always gets along well with people. This does not mean that she is necessarily a "hail fellow well met," a gregarious person with a warm handshake and a commanding voice. Some outstanding leaders are quiet and introspective, without any of the outward signs of personal power. Yet people follow these leaders willingly, accept their decisions, and admire them as leaders.

Sales managers, sociologists, psychologists, and political analysts often point out the difficulty of predicting personal appeal on the basis of outward appearances. One sales manager tells the story of a woman who come to him looking for a job. The woman was small, meek, and ill at ease; her voice was high-pitched, and her clothes looked af if they might have come from a Salvation Army fire sale. "Do you really think you can sell?" asked the sales manager?" "Yes, I do," replied the applicant, staring at her feet. Because a new salesperson was desperately needed, the manager decided to take a chance. "All right," he said, "you're hired." Today the woman is one of the five top salespeople out of nearly two hundred. And her customers think very highly of her. "No nonsense about Kay," they say. "A nice, down-to-earth, honest person."

Getting along with people, then, doesn't always mean having a sparkling line of chatter or an active membership in local clubs. It means having the kind of personality that, *for the kind of work you do,* makes it easy for you to get along *with the people you work with.*

It goes without saying, perhaps, that the leader must like and respect his subordinates. She must give them a feeling of accomplishment and recognize their growth potential. Beyond that it is pretty hard to generalize. The most diverse kinds of people sometimes succeed in the same kind of work.

THE VALUE OF INSIGHT ═══════════════

Insight is one reason that introspective people, despite their surface disadvantages, frequently become leaders. An individual who understands himself has a real head start in understanding others. He knows why he acts as he does, and consequently he can understand why others act as they do. He knows his own motivations and thus can appreciate the motivations of others.

Insight, strangely enough, does not correlate very well with intelligence. Many highly intelligent people have little insight into the minds and hearts of others. A fair number of rather limited men and women, on the other hand, appear to have remarkable insight. They know instinctively how others will react to what they say or do.

Whether insight can be improved or not is a moot question. Those of the positive-thinking school believe it can, while many industrial psychologists think it cannot. All of them agree, however, that insight into the words, actions, and goals of others is a common attribute of effective leaders.

PLANNING AND ORGANIZING

A famous cartoon shows two men sitting in an office with their feet on their desks. The desks are stacked with papers, and the floor is littered with things that have apparently fallen off the desks. One man is saying to the other, "Someday we've got to get organized."

And so they do, too, if they ever expect to get anything done. A leader is expected to plan and organize, not only her own work but to some extent the work of her subordinates. An office or a classroom or a home that is run by a person who can plan and organize is totally different from one run by a disorganized individual. Some companies even demand that desks be entirely cleared every night, presumably on the theory that this will instill a sense of order in their employees.

Learning how to plan and organize is not difficult. Actually doing it, though, is a bit harder. The fact is that many people will not plan and organize their work even though they know how, and even though they recognize its importance. Perhaps it's a quirk of human nature, an ingrown aversion to regimentation.

A person who aspires to leadership must drive herself to plan and organize. She must then make sure that the plans are carried out. Unless she does so, her situation will soon be chaotic. The work will pile up and both the leader and her subordinates will stare in dismay at the accumulation. "There's so much here," they will think, "that it's almost pointless to begin"—and so they don't begin. Or, they attack the job in illogical order—easiest things first, harder things next, hardest things never. Which clearly is not the way to get ahead.

CAN YOU DELEGATE AUTHORITY?

A leader who cannot delegate authority is no leader at all. He or she is an overworked, underpaid, one-person army. There are countless people like this in positions of responsibility. They try to do all of their work and a sizable part of their subordinates' work. It usually can't be done, with the consequence that the hardest-working person in the organization is one of the least efficient.

Part of the problem is that the nominal leader doesn't trust his subordinates. He may once have done the very jobs they are doing. No doubt he was very good at these jobs, and as a result earned a promotion. But he now looks at his subordinates' work and thinks, "I could do this a lot better." So he proceeds to do it, even though it's not part of his present responsibility. The outcome is lowered efficiency, hard feelings, and possibly a heart attack for the leader.

An effective leader delegates every bit of authority that can safely be delegated. She chooses subordinates wisely and then trusts them to the hilt. She takes the blame for their mistakes, of course, but they know it and try hard to avoid mistakes. She also gets some of the credit for their achievements, which she richly deserves. She is a true leader.

Can you delegate authority? Don't say "Certainly I can" unless you've tried it. Like setting personal goals, it looks like a cinch, but many intelligent and otherwise capable people can't do it. Perhaps they are perfectionists. Or perhaps they are unsure of themselves as leaders. In any event, the delegation of authority is a more delicate art than it may appear. It takes sound judgment, faith in others, and, most of all, a certain amount of cold nerve.

LEADERS ARE ALSO FOLLOWERS

In most cases, a person achieves a position of leadership partly because she was able to follow orders as a subordinate. Although she stood out from her fellow workers, she probably did not stand out because she was mulish and refused to accept advice or direction. She knew what was expected of her and she did it. Consequently, as a leader she usually does not find it hard to take orders from people who are still her superiors.

In addition to taking orders, the leader is generally able to accept advice, or even to seek advice if that is necessary. One of the characteristics of a leader is that she knows when she needs more information before taking action. She is not afraid to go out and get it, from the president, from her immediate superior, from an equal, or from the newest person in the organization

COMMUNICATION IS VITAL

Communication is a word that often appears in discussions of leadership. Communication in a large company is an extremely complex matter. There are many leaders on many levels, and unless the company has consistently and carefully fostered effective communication, the individual leader is likely to feel himself caught in a to-hell-with-the-other-guy web from which there is no escape.

In a similar organization, communication is a less serious problem. Unless the leaders are utterly unable to say what they mean, either orally or in writing, most of their subordinates will know the score.

YOU MUST GROW ON THE JOB

A leader who does not grow on the job ceases to be a leader. Such remarks as "I can't keep up with the youngsters any more" or "You can't teach an old dog new tricks" are frank confessions of defeat. Less frank but more insidious are comments like, "I've learned all I can in this position," or, "My job has no real challenges."

Leaders never lack challenges on the job, never stop growing in their present positions. They realize that the more they can learn now, the more ready they will be to step into a higher job when it is offered. They look forward to future challenges, but they do not bemoan the lack of present challenges. It is axiomatic that leaders make their own opportunities. One way of making them is to keep growing, learning, and striving to excel.

THE "PERFECT" LEADER

While there is no such thing as a perfect leader, there are certainly some very good leaders in all areas of modern life. You have seen many such people. You can hardly miss them, for they stand out unmistakably from the crowd.

What is it that makes them stand out? First, it is their broad range of talents. The leader who has even five or six of the fourteen traits listed on pages 164–165 is a remarkably capable person. If, in addition to these traits, he or she has some or all of the skills of power thinking, as described in the rest of this book, then he or she is a brilliantly endowed individual.

But more important than his separate accomplishments, perhaps, is his ability to blend all of these accomplishments into an integrated whole. For a person is not so much the *sum* of parts as an *amalgam* of those parts. He does not turn off one talent and turn on another one. Instead, he uses them all concurrently. He blends them. He has what most people would call *finesse*.

Can you develop finesse? I think you can. As a college professor, I have seen a great many students. It would be an oversimplification to say that these students come to college as impressionable boys and girls and leave as sophisticated young men and women. Many of them don't. But, then again, some of them do. As the brighter students acquire more and more skills, more and more knowledge, they really do change perceptibly. Success leads to success. They gain confidence; and some of them leave college with what looks to me very much like finesse.

I believe that people who are out of school can do the same thing. That is one of the purposes of *Mental Dynamics*: to show its readers how to learn, how to remember, how to think critically and creatively, and how to become the leaders of tomorrow.

TOMORROW'S LEADERS

A great deal of ground has been covered in this book. Some very profound subjects have been touched upon only lightly. It is important, surely, to learn more, to remember better, to think more logically and creatively. But it is of even greater importance to put these skills to constructive use. If leadership is the highest goal of a power thinker, then the highest goal of leadership unquestionably is to create a better life for yourself, your family, your friends, your business associates, and the world around you. That is the real goal for tomorrow's leaders.

The fourteenth mark of leadership is worth repeating verbatim: "The leader has a well-defined set of values. She knows what she wants *from* life, but she also knows what she should contribute *to* life. She has a sense of responsibility—personal, professional, local, national, and international."

TEN POINTERS FOR DEVELOPING PERSONAL POWER THROUGH LEADERSHIP

1. Set realistic personal goals. Remember that motivation is essential to success.

2. Recognize your own strengths and weaknesses. Build on your strengths. Try to correct your weaknesses.

3. Have confidence in your ability to lead. If a crisis arises, keep cool.

4. Combine decisiveness with sound judgment. Dare to make decisions, but be sure to make them on a sound, rational basis.

5. Work hard on human relations. Concentrate on getting along with people; use insight in dealing with them.

6. Plan and organize your work effectively. Once you have made your plans, carry them out promptly and efficiently.

7. Know how to be a good follower as well as a good leader.

8. Learn how to delegate authority. Once you have given a subordinate an assignment, trust him or her to carry it out.

9. Be clear and honest in communicating with both superiors and subordinates. Keep them informed about what is being done.

10. Grow continually on your job. Seek new challenges and new opportunities in it. Be prepared to accept larger responsibilities.

Appendix

Reading-Speed Scores

The Whys and Hows of Intelligent Skimming, pages 44–45.

461 words:

30 seconds	— 922 words a minute
45 seconds	— 691 words a minute
1 minute	— 461 words a minute
1 minute 15 seconds	— 403 words a minute
1 minute 30 seconds	— 345 words a minute
1 minute 45 seconds	— 288 words a minute
2 minutes	— 230 words a minute
2 minutes 15 seconds	— 192 words a minute — score
2 minutes 30 seconds	— 154 words a minute _____

Reading for the Main Idea, pages 44–45.

286 words:

20 seconds	— 858 words a minute
30 seconds	— 572 words a minute
45 seconds	— 429 words a minute
1 minute	— 286 words a minute
1 minute 15 seconds	— 251 words a minute
1 minute 30 seconds	— 215 words a minute
1 minute 45 seconds	— 178 words a minute — score
2 minutes	— 143 words a minute _____

Index